METAPHOR, CULTURE, AND WORLDVIEW

The Case of American English and the Chinese Language

Dilin Liu

University Press of America,® Inc.
Lanham · New York · Oxford

Copyright © 2002 by
University Press of America,® Inc.
4501 Forbes Boulevard
Suite 200
Lanham, Maryland 20706
UPA Acquisitions Department (301) 459-3366

PO Box 317
Oxford
OX2 9RU, UK

All rights reserved
Printed in the United States of America
British Library Cataloging in Publication Information Available

Library of Congress Cataloging-in-Publication Data

Liu, Dilin.
Metaphor, culture, and worldview : the case of American English
and the Chinese language / Dilin Liu.
p. cm
Includes bibliographical references (p.) and index.
1. English language—United States—Idioms. 2. English language—
Grammar, Comparative—Chinese. 3. English language—
United States—Terms and phrases. 4. Chinese language—
Grammar, Comparative—English. 5. Chinese language—
Idioms. 6. Figures of speech. 7. Americanisms.
8. Metaphor. I. Title.
PE2827 .L58 2002
428'.00973—dc21   2002032330 CIP

ISBN 0-7618-2422-7 (paperback : alk. ppr.)

∞™ The paper used in this publication meets the minimum
requirements of American National Standard for Information
Sciences—Permanence of Paper for Printed Library Materials,
ANSI Z39.48—1984

To Yun and Kan

Contents

Preface		vii
Acknowledgements		xi
Notes on Chinese Names and Translations		xiii
Chapter 1	Metaphor and Culture: An Introduction	1
Chapter 2	*Playing on Each Other's Turf*: Conflation of Sports, Business, and Politics in America	13
Chapter 3	*Playing Hardball* and *Hitting for Knockouts*: The Hard-fought Games between the Republicans and Clinton/the Democrats	27
Chapter 4	*Fumbles* in Wall Street and the *Three Strikes and You're Out* Law: The Use of Sports Metaphor in Other Areas of American Life	39
Chapter 5	*Buying an Argument* and *Selling an Agenda* in *Retail Politics*: Business Metaphors in American English	49
Chapter 6	*Dangjia* [M*anaging Family*] and *Chiku* [*Eating Bitterness*] at Work: Family and Eating in Chinese Culture and Language	55
Chapter 7	*Relatives or neighbors* and *married-out daughters*:	73

	Relationships between Mainland China and Taiwan, and Ties between China and the Overseas Chinese	
Chapter 8	*Human-eating society* and *Case-eating police*: The Use of Eating Metaphors in Chinese	87
Chapter 9	*Spinning Wheels* in English and *Singing Red and White Ffaces* in Chinese: More Culture-Specific Metaphors	101
Chapter 10	*Drop the Ball* vs. *Za Guo Le* [*Break the Cooking Pot*]: A Comparison of Cultural Views and Cross-Language Influence in Metaphor Use	111
Conclusion		119
List of Expressions of Dominant Metaphors		121
References		137
Index		147

Preface

As a linguist and an immigrant in America, I have been sensitive to Americans' use of language, especially the idioms they use. In the first few years after my arrival (I came to the U.S. in 1985,) I was sometimes puzzled by some of the idioms, especially those ubiquitous sports idioms such as "off base," "strike out," and "touch base with someone." I found such expressions difficult to follow because I didn't have the cultural knowledge behind them. Yet soon, I became used to them, and, more importantly, I have become fascinated by Americans' extensive use of sports jargon and their habitual conflation of sports with politics, business, personal life, etc. Simultaneously, I have been equally amazed at Americans' unconsciousness of such use and of their unawareness of the importance of sports knowledge in American public discourse[1]. Such a fascination and amazement have led me to a close examination of Americans' use of sports metaphors, and the effort has resulted in a couple of published articles on the issue (1996 and 2000). While researching Americans' use of sports metaphors, I developed a great interest in metaphor use in general, especially the dominant metaphors in both American English and the Chinese language, my native tongue. Soon I began to realize that, like American English, Chinese has its own unique metaphorical idioms like eating metaphors such as *eating vinegar* [being jealous] and *eating fragrance* [being popular], and these idioms, too, may present difficulty to speakers of other languages.

For almost a decade now, I have been exploring, among other questions, what metaphors the speakers of American English and Chinese often use, and why and how they use them. These issues constitute the foundation of this book. My intention of writing this book, the idea of which originated in the mid 1990s, has always been to offer a comparative study of the dominant metaphors in the two languages, a study that would be of help to professionals and students alike who are involved in studying American English or Chinese as a second or foreign language, Sina-American relationships, intercultural communication, and linguistics in general.

To collect materials for the book, I have paid close attention to the use of metaphors whenever I listen and read in the two languages. Such close listening and reading are accompanied by lengthy reflections and explorations of the meanings, functions, the sources, etc. of the metaphorical expressions identified. On many occasions, I have consulted colleagues and friends and reference books to accomplish my goal. In the process, I have learned to understand more and more that, although Americans and Chinese share some metaphors, there is a significant difference between the metaphors they use. While Americans tend to use significantly more sports, business, and driving metaphors among others, Chinese appear to use far more frequently family, eating, and acting metaphors.

Then why is there such a difference? My longtime interest and reading in anthropo- and socio-linguistics have directed me from the very beginning to cultural differences between the two languages. As many scholars have shown, language and culture are closely interwoven. Being a figure of speech, metaphor must also be simultaneously influenced by and actively influencing culture. This book will attempt to demonstrate this relationship by establishing the connections between the popular cultural activities and the dominant metaphors derived from these activities in the two respective cultures, such as the connection between Americans' mania for sports and the prominent use of sports metaphor in America, and between the Chinese obsession with eating and the omnipresence of eating metaphors in the Chinese language. In other words, the main purpose of this book is to argue, via examples from American English and the Chinese language and their respective cultures, that metaphor is a cultural product and the use of metaphors is largely culture-specific. As such, metaphor not only reveals but also shapes the speakers' worldviews and behavior.

Specifically, in Chapter 1, I will try to provide the theoretical foundation for the book by arguing the importance of metaphor in human thinking and communication and the close relationship between metaphor and culture. Then, in chapters 2 through 5, via examples from the media and other public speeches and writings, I will show that sports and business constitute the dominant metaphors in American English. The discussion aims to exhibit that the American use of sports and business metaphors is infused with a special American flavor. It radiates with a taste of the American experience, a spice of the American psyche, and a relish of the American vision. This close look at Americans' conflation of sports, business, politics, etc. shall leave the impression that life in America is, perhaps, a sport business in essence. Chapters 6 through 8 will illustrate that family and eating form the prevailing metaphors in Chinese. These chapters will demonstrate how Chinese conflate family/eating with politics, business, etc., and such a conflation in turn suggests that life in China is to an extent a family banquet in nature. To help further show that metaphor is culture-specific, Chapter 9 will explore the use of driving metaphor in English as a result of the easy accessibility of automobiles in America and the use of Beijing opera/acting metaphor in the Chinese language thanks to the opera's popularity in Chinese history. Chapter 10 will render a comparison and contrast of some English sports/business metaphors with some Chinese eating and family metaphors that are used to describe the same human behavior or phenomena. Such comparison will help pinpoint and highlight the differences between the world views of the speakers of the two languages. The chapter will also briefly discuss the influence of the two languages upon each other in terms of the use of metaphors by providing a list of Chinese and English metaphors that have transferred from one language to the other.

As a reference to help the reader better grasp the dominant metaphors discussed in the book, I have provided at the end of the book a glossary of dominant metaphorical idioms derived from the various metaphors discussed in the book including sports, business, and driving metaphors in American English, and family, eating, and Beijing opera/acting metaphors in Chinese. Each entry contains a definition of both the expression's literal and figurative meanings. This glossary should be of special use to professionals and students who are learning either English or Chinese as a second/ foreign language or who are studying or engaged in the study of Sina-American relations.

To conclude my preface, I would like to express my gratitude to the individuals who have helped and/or supported me in this book project. First I would like to thank Bryan Farha for providing me with a lot of valuable information on American sports idioms. I then want to express my appreciation to Eric Meyer and Mat Randall for their close proofreading of the drafts of the manuscript and for the critical comments they made, though any remaining errors are mine only. I would also like to thank the UPA staff for the consultation they gave me on issues such as the preparation of the camera-ready copy of the manuscript and the obtaining of copyright permissions. Of course, my greatest gratitude goes to my dear wife, Yun Fu, for her never ending encouragement and support, and for her patience during my busy hours working on this book and my other writing projects.

Notes

1. For example, E.D. Hirsch, a renowned American scholar on American culture, and his colleagues Kett, and Trefil (1993) have basically neglected sports in their famous *Dictionary of Cultural Literacy.* The dictionary supposedly contains all the necessary information and knowledge that an American needs to possess in order to function adequately in society. Yet while the dictionary contains sections such as "Earth Sciences," "Fine Arts," "Medicine," "politics," and "Proverbs," it fails to include a section on sports or sports jargon and idioms. Out of the approximately 7,500 entries, only about 20 are related to sports. Moreover, whereas one can locate, in its "Idioms" section, expressions like "ghost town" and "lip service" whose meaning is rather self-evident, one cannot find any of the extensively used sports idioms whose figurative meaning is not very transparent such as "call an audible," "out in left field," and "strike out." If renowned scholars on language and culture do not understand the eminence of sports metaphors in American English, how do we expect the general public to do so?

Acknowledgements

I would like to express my gratitude to the following publishers or other copyright owners for allowing me to reproduce their materials: the *Daily Oklahoman*: various quotes; Greenwood Publishing Group: some materials from Liu, D. & Lin, C. (1999), "The pride of *Zuguo:* China's perennial appeal to the overseas Chinese and an emergent civic discourse in a global community," in Randy Cluver and John Powers (Eds), *Civic discourse, civil society, and Chinese communities* (pp.209-220), Stamford, CT: Ablex; Indiana University Press: excerpts from Lu Xun's "A Madman's Diary; Louis Rukeyser of the Maryland Public Television's *Wall $treet Week with Louis Rukeyser* program: excerpts from two of the shows; *Time* magazine for the "Still Standing" picture caption.

Although every effort has been made to acknowledge published materials used in this book whenever the source can be traced, the author apologizes for any errors or omissions in the above list of acknowledgement, and would be grateful to be notified of any corrections that should be incorporated in the next edition or reprint of this book.

Notes on Chinese names and translations

There are several systems used in the English translation of Chinese names, e.g. the "pinyin" translation, a roman spelling system currently used in Mainland China and most international publications, and the "Wade-Giles" system popular before the 1990s and still used in Taiwan. In this book, I have opted to use pinyin for all Chinese names including the names of individuals from Taiwan and other parts of the world except for those Taiwanese and overseas Chinese who have established "Wade-Giles" translations in the international media because of their publicity such as Lee Teng-hui, the former leader of Taiwan, and Lee Kuan Yew, the former leader of Singapore. The exceptions are given to these well-known names in order to avoid any confusion that might be caused by using a different translation system.

In discussing the use of metaphors in the Chinese language, I have cited many examples from Chinese rendered in English translation. Except for the excerpts from Luxun's "A Madman's Story" (translated by Yang Xianyi and Gladys Yang) cited in Chapter 8, all the English translations of Chinese publications in this book are mine. Again I used pinyin in all the translations and I consulted *Han Ying Cidian* [A *Chinese-English Dictionary*] in determining the word boundaries while translating all the Chinese words that consist of more than two Chinese characters.

Chapter 1

Metaphor and Culture—An Introduction

"In the business of diplomacy, you often *score runs by hitting singles.* And I think the President [Clinton] and President Yeltsin *hit a series of good solid singles that'll add up to scoring a great many runs.*"
--Warren Christopher, former Secretary of State, responding to Republicans' criticism of President Clinton's 1995 visit to Moscow as being a waste of time and money.

"We [Beijing government] will respect the way of life of our *Tongbao* ("descendants born to the same parents") in Taiwan and respect their wish to *danjia zuozhu* ("manage [their] family and be [their own] masters") and safeguard all the legitimate rights of the *tongbao* in Taiwan. . . . People on both sides [of the Taiwan Strait] are Chinese, so there is *no shui chi shui de wenti* [no such an issue as who eats up who]"
--Qian Qichen, Chinese Vice Premier in charge of Foreign affairs, on the issue of the unification between Beijing and Taiwan

Any close scrutiny of human communication, ancient or contemporary, formal or informal, will reveal the popularity of metaphor. However, as Fiumara (1995) states, "the topic of metaphor has been systematically ignored throughout centuries" (p. 4). The culprit for this neglect may be our schizophrenia towards metaphor. Historically, many scholars and thinkers have, on the one hand, exhibited a strong antipathy towards metaphor, denouncing it either as an unnecessary pomp that introduces ambiguity or as a scheme that corrupts truth. Yet, on the other hand, in the process of making their argument against metaphor, they often resort to nothing other than metaphor itself.¹ Plato, a founding father of Western philosophy and a staunch foe of metaphor, provides a good example. In the *Phaedo*, Plato dismisses corporeal senses, the mechanism through which metaphor often operates, as unfit for understanding truth and contends that one can attain truth only through *el lkpivns* [pure and unadulterated] thought (*Collected Dialogues*, p. 48). But the word *el lkpivns* in Greek literally means "unmixed, without alloy." So used, the word presents a corporeal image for pureness, hence a metaphor in process. Such use of metaphor is not an accident or exception in Plato's works. The expression of "written on the soul of the listener" in the *Phaedrus* (*Collected Dialogues*, p. 523) and the statement that "imitation is a kind of a game" in the *Republic* (p. 273) are just two more examples. In the *Phaedrus*, Socrates is preaching the purity of speech and condemning writing for the lack of it, yet to support his point, he uses a writing metaphor by comparing spoken truth to be something "written on the soul of the listener." In so doing, Socrates manages only to demonstrate the indispensability of metaphor and perhaps also writing, ironic as it may sound. Similarly, the definition of imitation as a "game" serves only to show the vitality of metaphor.

Since the 1970s, quite a few studies (Fauconnier, 1994, 1997; Fiumara, 1995; Gibbs, 1994, 1996; Gibbs and Steem, 1999; Goatly, 1997; Lakoff, 1987, 1990; Lakoff and Johnson, 1980; Lakoff and Turner, 1989) have challenged, directly or indirectly, this traditional bias towards metaphor and managed to show that metaphor is fundamental to the human thinking process. Yet the traditional contradictory attitude towards metaphor, as Fiumara (1995) argues, still affects the contemporary human mentality and "represents a general cognitive predicament: humans appear to be constantly engaged in striving to optimize the equilibrium between their ineliminable metaphoricity and literalness" (p. 4). Hardaway's (1976) attack on the use of sports metaphor best illustrates this point. After seriously criticizing the use of sports metaphor as "public doublespeak in America," she nonetheless knowingly concludes her essay with a sports metaphor herself: "It is at least worth a few minutes of our time to wrestle (there it is again) with the decision of whether we really want to see ourselves forever as a nation of team players and sports fans" (p. 82). The biggest irony here is that, as revealed in her parenthesis comments "there it is again," she was fully aware that she was doing the same thing that she was criticizing others for doing, but she appeared to have no other choice.

Hardaway's practice only highlights the indispensability of metaphor. It is rather clear that the use of metaphor is not just a matter of choice of expressions nor is it merely a rhetorical device or a linguistic convenience in human communication. "Far from being a mere matter of ornament, it [metaphor] participates fully in the progress of knowledge: in replacing some stale `natural' kinds with novel and illuminating categories. . . and in bringing us new worlds" (Goodman, 1981, p. 175). In other words, "metaphor and the mental processes it entails," to cite Goatly (1997, p. 1), "are basic to language and cognition." More importantly, metaphor "is a significant part of people's everyday conceptual systems" (Gibbs and Steen, 1999, p. 2). It is, as Lakoff and Johnson (1980) argue, an indispensable means through which human beings think and act:

> [M]any people think they can get along perfectly well without metaphor. We have found, on the contrary, that metaphor is pervasive in everyday life, not just in language but in thought and action. Our ordinary conceptual system, in terms of which we both think and act, is fundamentally metaphorical in nature. (p. 3)

Take Americans for example. Consciously or unconsciously, Americans view their life as sport and think and act accordingly. Whether it is politics, business, or even personal relationships, it is a game for Americans to win. Politicians *fight* and *compete* with their opponents in order to *win* an election. Business people have to *beat* their *competitors* to survive. Even in daily chores and personal relationships, people are playing games, for they often *touch base with each other,* and they like to *score points* on a date, yet they sometimes still *strike out* in their effort. In other words, Americans frequently discuss their activities in terms of sports: baseball, boxing, football, etc. It is no wonder that the word *race* is a far better known term for "election campaign" and the phrase "*running* mate" sounds far more familiar than that of someone's "campaign partner." Similarly, the declaration "We *beat* their offer" surely sounds more American than "We made a better offer than theirs," and the statement "We *scored a home-run* in the *deal*" rings dearer in American business than "We made important progress in the business transaction."

Metaphor not only reflects but also shapes our conceptual system. It is often through the metaphorical process that human beings conceptualize the world and construct reality. Kövecses (1999), Leondar (1975), and Muhlhausler (1995) both argue and show that to understand things alien or new, human beings always first resort to metaphor. In fact, certain "abstract concepts can only emerge metaphorically" (Kövecses, 1999, p. 187). Also we constantly name novel concepts or newly invented products metaphorically, or in Aristotle's words, we use "metaphors to give names to nameless things" (*Rhetoric*, p. 1405a).

For instance, we call the electronic communication system internet *cyberspace super highway* where people can *visit* various *sites* and send and receive *mail*. A new and non-spatial system is thus understood via a comparison to some traditional physical objects and concepts. "Of course once such a newly discovered phenomenon is well understood and extricated from its original context, the metaphor will vanish into the literal context, its heuristic work completed"(Fiumara, p. 12). Few Americans consider these internet terms metaphorical. By the same token, still fewer regard "a political *race*" or "*sell* an idea" as a metaphor when they use such expressions. Via the metaphorical process, new concepts or phenomena have become literal and, therefore, real. In the process of conceptualizing or re-conceptualizing the world, metaphor leads us to new understandings and new discoveries. Even Aristotle seems to appreciate such function of metaphor when he writes in the *Rhetoric*, "It is from metaphor that we can best get hold of something fresh" (p. 1410a). In fact, as Muhlhausler (1995) suggests, "Most advances in the sciences are a consequence of the adoption of new metaphorical interpretations" (p. 281). For example, the metaphor of *cloning* life and the concept of *starving* cancer cells as a treatment of the disease have become or are in the process of becoming reality.

Although the use of metaphor is universal, the choice of specific metaphors for interpreting the world is frequently culture-specific. Many scholars (Fantini, 1995; Hymes, 1972; Wierzbicka 1991, 1992; Whorf, 1956) have shown that language is a cultural product. Although few scholars today embrace linguistic determinism, most still believe, to various degrees, in linguistic relativity and agree that "language, culture and meaning have inextricably contaminated each other" (Hill and Mannheim, 1992, pp. 382-383). More than grammatical structure and some other aspects of language, metaphor, like vocabulary, is especially culture-bound. This is because the metaphorical process is one of mapping an understanding of one domain, often a common physical or perceptual experience, onto another domain of knowledge, frequently an abstract one. As Gibbs (1999), Kovesces (1999), and Emanatian (1999) demonstrate, the metaphors we choose to help understand and depict the world are to a great extent related to and perhaps determined by our life experience. As a result, it is not uncommon that speakers of one language find it hard to appreciate the metaphors of another language. This is because "communication is based on the same conceptual system that we use in thinking and acting" (Lakoff and Johnson, 1980, p. 3). It is also due to the way metaphor works: "metaphor renders the truth of experience as the truth of knowledge to an established public world" (Shiff, 1981, p. 106). Thus, individuals who do not live in the same established world or speech community will sometimes possess rather different conceptual systems and will in turn find each other's metaphors sometimes difficult to understand. Moreover, since "our conceptual system is not something we are normally aware of"(Lakoff and Johnson, 1980, p. 3), we tend to overlook this potential problem when using metaphors to communicate with speakers of other languages.

The first epigraph at the beginning of the chapter provides a good example. It was a statement that former Secretary of State Warren Christopher made at a May 11, 1995 press conference in Kiev, Ukraine (the statement cited from "White House defends talks," p. A2). He was accompanying President Clinton on a visit to some of the former Soviet republics, and they had just completed a visit to Moscow. He made the comments in response to the Republican Party's criticism that their visit was a waste of time and money since it had accomplished very little. In his statement, Christopher used a baseball metaphor to suggest that, despite lack of apparent breakthroughs, Clinton's visit was a success because conducting diplomacy was like playing baseball where winning or attaining objectives was often achieved by making a small step at a time, and these small steps would eventually lead to breakthroughs. He did not explain the metaphor nor did he elaborate on his point at the conference. A more significant but less noticeable fact is that he made the analogy in a metaphor, not a simile. Although metaphor and simile are both figurative uses of language relying on analogy, the two differ significantly. A simile expresses an analogy by the structure of "A is or functions *like* or *as* B" and, in doing so, it openly acknowledges the fundamental difference between A and B while showing their similarities. A metaphor, on the other hand, renders an analogy by the "A *is* B" structure." As such, it hides the comparison in progress and suppresses the difference between the two matters being compared. In other words, simile shows resemblance but metaphor expresses *identity* between two different things.

Christopher's choice of metaphor over simile was no accident. Metaphor, not simile, is the norm when it comes to the use of sports jargon in America. Such practice, as I will argue in Chapter 2, results from and, simultaneously, points to two important facts. Americans love sports so much and use sports metaphors so frequently that sports knowledge has become an established part of American cultural literacy. Second, in the process of this constant use of sports metaphor, Americans, consciously or unconsciously, conflate sports with other activities, making life a sport indeed, and hence making simile a redundant figure of speech when it comes to the use of sports metaphor. To the American audience, Christopher did not need to offer an explanation of the metaphor in making his comments. However, made at an international news conference, his statement had left many in the audience wondering, to say the least, what it meant since baseball is not even played in many other countries, and, more importantly, even in countries where it is, baseball metaphor claims no popularity, certainly not to the degree in America.

To show another example of metaphor being culture-bond, let us read the English translation of a passage from a June 6, 1996 front-page article in *Shijie Zhoukan* (the weekly magazine of *Shijie Ribao*, the largest Chinese newspaper in America). The author of the article, Zeng Huiyan, was criticizing many Mainland Chinese in America for forgetting the people who had fought and died in the 1989 Tiananmen Crackdown. After stating that the Chinese who were still commemorating the anniversary of the event were mostly from Hong Kong and Taiwan, she wrote, "yet those who were shot and killed were Mainland Chinese. Hundreds of thousands *who ate steamed bread soaked in blood* are also Mainland Chinese" (italics added; p. S1).[2] The expression of "ate steamed bread soaked with blood" would surely perplex non-Chinese speakers. Yet to Chinese, it is just one of the many eating metaphors they use daily. "Eating steamed bread soaked with blood" means "benefiting from the tragedy of other people's suffering and deaths." In the present case, the author was referring to the fact that after the Tiananmen Crackdown, the American government passed a bill to protect Chinese nationals in the U. S. from possible persecution in China by allowing them to remain permanently and, as a result, many Chinese (more than 80,000) acquired Permanent Resident status (the commonly known Green Card).

That eating metaphors in Chinese often puzzle and also fascinate speakers of other languages can also be seen in Alexander Wolfe's essay in the July 22, 1996 issue of *Sports Illustrated*. In this report prepared before the Atlanta Olympics Games and based on his visit and interviews conducted in China, Wolfe tried to explain the recent great success of Chinese female athletes. He writes, "The applicable phrase here is *chi ku*: eating bitterness," and he goes on to quote a Chinese official in charge of sports as saying "Chinese women are better able to eat bitterness and endure hardships than Western women" (p. 156). Wolfe did not immediately explain the phrase *eat bitterness*, a metaphor that means "work hard by willingly suffering pain and other afflictions." The reader has to figure out the meaning by finishing the life stories of a few incredibly hard- working Chinese female athletes Wolfe told in the report. In other words, the reader has to garner its meaning from the context.

It is important to point out, however, that while metaphors are often culture-specific, they are not culture-exclusive. Carroll's (1963) discussion on linguistic relativity may help explain this seemingly somewhat paradoxical statement: "The speakers of one language . . . .may tend to ignore differences which are regularly noticed by the speakers of another language. This is not to say that they *always* ignore them, for these differences can indeed be recognized and talked about in any language, but they are differences which are not always salient in their experiences" (p. 12). Of course, it would make more sense for the sake of discussion of metaphor if we *change* the word "differences" in the quote to "similarities." Metaphors that work on similarities *salient* in one language can and may be used in another language where the similarities are less salient, but they will be far less frequently used. So while the above examples from American English and Chinese help illustrate the difficulty one may encounter in understanding other people's metaphors, such examples do not suggest that speakers of different languages never use the same type of metaphor. In fact, they do. Americans sometimes employ eating metaphors such as "It's a piece of cake" to mean an easy job; Chinese occasionally make use of sports metaphor such as "One cannot learn to swim in shallow water" (meaning one has to take on difficult tasks to learn the skills needed).

Yet an examination of metaphor usage in American English and the Chinese language will show that eating is a dominant metaphor in Chinese but not in America, and sport is a dominant metaphor in America but not in China. No other metaphors are more widely used in America than sports, especially in the public discourse. By the same token, in China sport as a metaphor plays a very limited role when compared to eating. In fact, as I will show in Chapter 2 and Chapter 6, some cultural models or the metaphorical processes in non-linguistic symbolic practices found in the two cultures also point to sports and business as important metaphorical forces in America, and family and eating as powerful metaphorical tools in China. The main reason is that while the similarities between sports and life in general are much more salient in America than in China, the opposite is true of the similarities between eating and life, a point that I will explore in depth in Chapters 2 and Chapter 6 respectively and in the rest of the book as well. Only metaphors that work on similarities salient in the speakers' experiences become dominant metaphors in their language. Dominant metaphors best manifest how the speakers of the language view the world and construct reality because the repeated use of a metaphor, while revealing the speakers' conceptual system and psyche, also constantly reinforces their worldview.

A juxtaposed examination of the use of metaphor in two different languages can highlight the dominant metaphors in the languages being examined and help us better appreciate the cultures and the peoples who speak the languages. A few simple comparative examples here will, I deem, shed some light on my point. First, what Americans often like to view as sports tend to be seen by Chinese in terms of family relationships and domestic events including cooking and eating. For instance, government leaders in America such as mayors, governors, and the President are constantly compared to sportsmen: they first have to *run for* and *win* the office in election and then to *play* and *score points* in political or legislature *games* and *fight* the opposition while in office. Yet government officials in China are often regarded as parents, as is shown in the term *fumu guan* meaning literally "father-mother officials." As such, they operate the government in a way similar to that of running and providing for a family. It is no wonder that Lao Zi (also known as Lao Tzu), a famous Chinese thinker as influential as Confucius, once said that "ruling a large country is like cooking a delicacy dish" (cited in Wang Jun, 2001), a task that requires great care and skills. Such conflation of family and government should not, however, come as a surprise in a country where the word "state" or "county" is *guojia,* whose literal meaning is "state-family" and where *gongjia* ["public family"] is frequently used to refer to the state.

Similarly, in asking the question who is really in charge at a place, Americans like to say "Who's *calling the shots*" but Chinese often utter "*shui dangjia?*" meaning "Who's *managing [the] family*." It may be of interest to note here that George Wehrfritz, in a 1995 *Newsweek* article about Chinese President Jiang Zemin's growing power and his distancing from his protector Deng Xiaoping, writes, "Jiang has also grown more hard-line, straying from a Dengist policy he once promised to uphold—and thereby showing that he, not Deng, now *calls the shots*" (italics mine; p. 35). Such an application of an American metaphor to a Chinese context, however fascinating, may seem somewhat comic to the Chinese as was the case when Deng Xiaoping donned a cowboy hat during his 1979 visit to America. Americans are not the only ones to use metaphors unique to their culture to describe other counties' politics.

In a news report about how Japanese Prime Minister Junichiro Koizumi made sure that his Foreign Affairs Minister Makiko Tanaka (the first female to hold such position in Japan and a feminist to a certain degree), understands that he, not she, is in charge and has the final say in all important foreign policies and foreign affairs personnel decisions, Chang Fang-Ming, a journalist from Taiwan's Central News Agency, used a Chinese family-metaphor to describe the situation. After the headline, "Prime Minister Koizumi taught the Foreign Affairs Minister Tanaka that "it is he who *dangjiao zuozhu* ("who manages the family and is the master"), the report states, "Japanese female Foreign Affairs Minister Makiko Tanaka failed in her attempt to challenge the Prime Minister in the appointment of high-level foreign affairs officials. The names for the position and the Ambassador to the U.S. were decided according to the Prime Minister's will. Prime Minister Koizumi has taught Foreign Affairs Minister Tanaka that it is he who "*dangjia zuozhu*" (Chang Fang-ming, 2001). As another contrast between the American and Chinese use of metaphors, what Americans like to see as business is likely to be viewed by Chinese as eating. For example, in expressing the idea of not believing or agreeing with what another person says or does, Americans often say "I don't *buy* that" whereas Chinese would utter "*wobuchi nineitao!*" meaning literally "I don't *eat* your type of practice/argument!" Also what Americans call "*cash in*" (taking advantage of something) is often referred to in Chinese as "*scooping oil water*, " meaning to grab the best part from a dish.

These few examples offer us a glimpse of how Americans and Chinese view the world and life differently. Such different views often lead to different attitudes and practicses in politics, business, education, and life in general. That is why it is important that we not only study "the metaphors we live by," a point Lakoff and Johnson (1981) convincingly presented almost two decades ago, but also, as Muhlhausler (1995) proposes, examine "the metaphors others live by." Only through such studies can we gain a better and more in-depth understanding and appreciation of speakers of other languages and seek more effective communication with them. For example, knowing that Chinese view a state or country as a family and that they regard officials as the all powerful patriarchs and citizens as children would surely make it easier to understand why the Chinese government vehemently contends that its treatment of its citizens is absolutely a domestic matter. Realizing that China is a country where for centuries life has been interpreted primarily as an event of eating helps better contextualize the Chinese government's argument that having enough to eat is the first and foremost human right. While I do not suggest that cultural beliefs are the main or the only reason for Beijing's stance and rhetoric, I do argue that they have played a role. Otherwise it will be difficult to explain why China has been the most prominent and perhaps the first country to employ and rely heavily on this argument in defending its human rights record when many poorer countries like Burma and some in Africa have not, at least not to the degree China has, in defending theirs.

By the same token, recognizing that America is a country founded largely on the ideal of free competition and fair play makes it easier to understand America's aggressive push for a free world economy. Such an understanding would perhaps also have made China feel less offended and worried when the Bush administration took office and defined the Sino-America relationship as "competitors." In America, the term "competitors" has long defined the relationship among businesses and many organizations and, more importantly, Americans consider competition among one another the way of life, a point I will elaborate and explore in the next chapter. Similarly in America, a country where life has also been perceived as business, the notion of "*selling*" an idea or a message " makes much better sense than in countries such as China where the concept of "selling" has traditionally been viewed more negatively. The rest of the book aims to render a discussion of the dominant metaphors in American English and the Chinese language that will help us not only understand the close relationship between metaphor and culture but also better appreciate other people's way of life and worldviews.

Notes

1. It is necessary to point out that not all Western scholars and thinkers disparage metaphor. Historically, there have been a few who hold a positive attitude towards metaphor including Aristotle. Commenting on the merits of metaphor, Aristotle writes, "Metaphor, moreover, gives style clearness, charm, and distinction as nothing else can. . ." (*Rhetoric*, p. 1404b).

2. This is an English translation. The translation is mine, and as I stated in the "Notes on Chinese names and translations," unless stated otherwise, the English translations of the cited Chinese statements and texts in the book are all mine.

Chapter 2

Playing on Each Other's Turf: Conflation of Sports, Business, and Politics in America[1]

> ". . . in the final round of the Republican versus Democratic *boxing match* . . ., [Ted Strickland, Ohio Democratic candidate for Congress, is engaged in] *retail politics*.. . .[and] is *banking on* help from a big name [Mrs. Hillary Clinton]."
> --"The President and the election," program of ABC's *Nightline* October 28, 1998

Although metaphorical use of sports and business jargon exists probably in all cultures, such use in America, I contend, stands out for its extensiveness and intensity and, more importantly, for its unique features that highlight both the American psyche and the American way of life. Any close look at Americans' speeches and writings will reveal that sports and business jargon permeates every facet of American life and imbues every medium of communication. Yet before I illustrate the ubiquitous use of these metaphors, which I will do in the three immediate following chapters, it is important and necessary to explore the causes of sports' unusual popularity and the importance of business in America and the reasons for Americans' conflation of sports, business, politics, and other aspects of life.

Few will perhaps dispute the overwhelming popularity of sports in America, for the Nielsen TV ratings "have consistently shown that sports outpoll politics and many other programs on almost any day" (Iso-Ahola and Hatfield, 1986, p. 5). In fact, as Roberts and Olson (1989, pp. vi-vii) point out, sports have taken the place of work, family, and religion as the focus of many Americans' lives, making sports a true "national obsession." The reasons for Americans' passion for sports are less obvious, however. Extensive research appears to suggest the following to be the main causes of Americans' obsession with sports: the inherent matching and integration of the spirit of sports with the essence of the American way of life, schools' inculcation, politicians' campaigns, and media and business's promotions.

The American way of life is best known or, to be more precise, is perceived as equality of opportunity, hard work, competition, and prosperity. Of these proclaimed American values, competition is perhaps the core. "Most Americans," as Eitzen and Sage (1993) point out, "believe it [competition] to be the one quality that has made America great because it motivates individuals and groups to be discontented with the status quo and with being second best" (p. 56). Of course, Americans do not believe simply in competition per se. They believe, more importantly, in the ideal of free competition for social/economic advancement and in the idea of individual responsibility for success or failure. This American ideology of free and open competition for success happens to be the creed (not necessarily the practice) of sports, particularly the creed of modern American sport, as Nixon (1984, pp. 19-20) contends. Since the perceived nature and principles of the American way of life are identical to those of sport, many Americans nurture the conviction that participation in sport not only helps them develop the personal attributes desirable in life, such as competitiveness, courage, discipline, and mental and physical fitness, but also provides them with a path to social/financial success, although the number of Americans who attain such success via sports may be minuscule in percentage.

Another aspect of the American ideology that has not received enough attention is the credo that, with hard work and strife, one can not only succeed but also be the best. In fact, success in America is often defined as being "the best" or "Number One." Every individual, every business, or every school is encouraged to strive to be the best, and many claim to be Number One. This creed of "being Number One" is also found or perhaps has its root in American sports, and *only* in American sports I dare to say. When people throughout the rest of the world participate in sports to compete, they do not have to be the best to be honored. They will be awarded as second, third, etc. In other words, people compete not just for the first place but also for other places since they will still be considered a winner. That is true in almost all international sports such as basketball and volleyball, where the places of one to twelve or even more will be decided. Even the Olympic Games honor the top three with gold, silver, and bronze metals. It is very different in American sports, however, especially in the major ball games where only the number one team is honored. There are no second, third, etc. places acknowledged in NBA, NFL, or the World Series. A team either has to win it all, or, no matter how many games it has won, it is not much different from those who lose it all. In this American system, without winning the Championship, the Superbowl, or the World Series, a team will remain largely obscure.

That is why the players of the teams entering the playoffs constantly sense the pressure to win it all. If they do not achieve that goal, they will feel like and/or will be treated as losers, despite the fact that they have accomplished so much by being in the playoffs. The comments of Antonio Davis, a player of the 1998 Indiana Pacers of the NBA, best illustrate the point. After their team lost (3 to 4 in a seven-game series) to the Chicago Bulls in the NBA's Eastern Conference finals, Davis said, "Nobody remembers that we took them to a seventh game and all that stuff. People only remember winners. What's the difference between Vancouver [the team with the worst record in NBA that year] and us? There's no difference. They're not winning, and we didn't win. *There's no room for second place* (italics for emphasis added; Nance, 1998, p. C3). By grouping his team, which had won the second place, with the team that had the worst record in NBA that season, Davis clearly reveals the American mentality that only the best counts. An Oklahoma State sports fan's letter to the Sports Editor of *Daily Oklahoman* (February 28, 1999, p. B3) expresses the same frame of mind:

> Ditch the "Final Four" Banner
> I am writing this letter after visiting with several proud OSU supporters. With the expansion of Gallagher-Iba Arena in progress, OSU could use the added ceiling spaces to do what is fair and right.
> As many people know, OSU has a great tradition of excellence in several sports. In fact, OSU has captured 42 (yes, 42) NCAA team championships. It is an awesome sight to walk into Gallagher-Iba Arena and see the masses of NCAA Championship banners that hang from the ceiling.

> But there is something else up there that disturbs me and many other OSU fans. The largest and most distinguished banner is not for an NCAA Championship. It is a nice large banner that signifiers OSU basketball's 1995 Final Four [being one of the final four teams in the tournament]. That was a great accomplishment, but worthy of a banner?
> *A banner should signify a victory and championship. Not merely placing in the top four. Don't lower the standards for a banner by recognizing near-misses. . . . OSU fans, don't settle for less! Don't be satisfied with getting close. Expect to win NCAA Championships.* And when that happens, you should add a banner. (Italics added; "Ditch the "Final Four" banner," B3, February 28, 1999).

This "being the best" American mentality has often turned everyday life into a sport game. People compete in almost everything. They compete in politics, business, and even in their personal life, as shown in young people's frequent boast about their achievement on a date: "I *got to first base* with her/him" or "I *hit a home run* with her/him".

American schools are another contributing factor to the American sports mania. While sports as extracurricular activities are universal, American schools' sports programs are unique and have no true counterparts in the rest of the world. There are very few high schools or colleges in America that do not have a sports program and, in many schools, athletics outweighs all other programs in terms of money and attention received.[2] An American school's reputation often rests largely on its sports program. In order to enroll top athletes to help their program, colleges not only offer special scholarships to athletes (sometimes even cheerleaders) but also provide them with privileges such as private academic tutoring, and sometimes, lower admission requirements. These and other special treatments are so common that they have become taken-for-granted practices to most Americans but not to international students. Quite a few international students at our school have asked me why, at the annual new students orientation camp, the athlete students are given a special introduction by the school authority while no other groups of students receive such an honor. Another puzzling American school practice is to cancel classes for celebration when the school wins a state or national sport championship, but awards in other areas including academia often do not receive even remotely comparable recognition. Academics being secondary to sports can be partially seen in the statement that an official from the Santa Fe High School in Edmond, Oklahoma, made after the school's academic team won the state annual Academic Bowl in 1998: "Winning a competition like this, Crittendon [the school official] said, is like winning a state championship in football" (Hartman, February 25, 1998, p. A9). The importance of sports over academia cannot be missed here because she was trying to compare the Academic Bowl to a state championship in football, something far better known and cherished by many people.

As a country, from the national to the local level, Americans go out of their way to honor athletes. Across the U.S., there are numerous streets that are named after famous athletes. As a recent example, on September 29, 1999, the Senate passed a resolution to rename St. Louis section of Interstate High Way 70 as Mark McGuire Highway after he set a homerun record in a season. This showering of honors onto athletes forms a sharp contrast with the lack or rarity of it in regard to heroes and unusual achievers in other fields. For instance, I am not aware of any street that is named after a Nobel Prize winner even though the contribution of the latter to mankind is surely not less, if not more, than any of the athletes. Also, while college and professional championship teams are routinely invited to meet the President in the White House, academic champions either seldom receive such honor or are not given much publicity in the media even when they do receive such honor. All the honors, privileges, and publicity that American athlete students receive have made sports particularly attractive to our young people and have fostered in our students a strong urge to become involved in sports, despite the fact that very few can make their school teams.

This urge is partly manifested in American youth's love affair with brand-name sportswear. It is perhaps a universal human nature to desire brand-name products, but it is basically an American phenomenon to be obsessed with brand-name sportswear. The stories of quite a few of my Chinese friends support this. When their children first came to the U.S., they wore to school the kind of casual or dress shoes they had worn to school in China, but only one semester afterwards, they all demanded brand-name athletic shoes such as Nike and Reebok because the children had been made to feel out of place in school with their out-of-style shoes and were pressured by their peers to change. One reason that American youth crave brand-name sportswear is, I believe, that wearing these shoes or clothes may serve as, among other things, a vicarious sports participation experience for many of the children who cannot make their school sports teams or join sports clubs.

American children's strong desire to be involved in sports can also be seen in many school girls' yearning to be cheerleaders at any cost (no one would forget the Texan mother who would commit murder to make her daughter a cheerleader). All this can be attributed to the American practice of measuring students' and schools' success, to a great extent, by gauging their achievements in sports. Such a practice constitutes in a way a cultural model of mapping one domain, sports, to another, education.

The tremendous popularity of sports in America has resulted in the public's great familiarity with sports jargon, which, in turn, has created the condition and environment for the broad use of sports terms in non-sport fields and activities. Examples of the figurative use of sports jargon cited earlier in the paper demonstrate clearly that sports metaphors are used by all Americans, regardless of class, profession, race, age, or gender. Sports jargon can be found in the speeches of the educated and the upper class like the President, Secretary of State, and the renowned economist Louis Rukeyser, and it also finds its way into ordinary citizens' everyday language. Sports jargon abounds in casual as well as formal speeches. Sports jargon is so pervasive and so widely spread that political and business activities and even American laws are better known in sports' terms for average Americans. An election campaign is known mostly as a "race" to "run." The crime bill to imprison for life repeated violent criminals is far better known as the "Three strikes and you're out" bill.

Strong American characteristics are found in both the way sports analogies and idioms are used in America and the way sports jargon functions in American life. The most noticeable feature of Americans' use of sports analogies is that, as I have already pointed out in the preceding chapter, the comparison of a non-sport activity/event to that of sport is rendered mostly in metaphor, a figure of speech where A is directly compared to B in the A-is-B structure. The comparison is seldom presented in simile, a figure of speech where A is said to be or to function *like* or *as* B. A very good example of Americans' preference of metaphor over simile in using sports metaphor can been seen in the following email message a colleague of mine wrote. The message was in response to another professor's comments regarding how to assess faculty for merit pay:

> The biggest can of worms I see with this is that faculty's salaries for NEXT year will be determined on the basis of their performance THIS year, using a process and criteria that were not announced until THIS

year was already over. *Isn't that like a teacher passing out a syllabus with grading criteria on the last day of class?* I think we're opening ourselves to many more complaints of unfairness than would be the case if we announced the rules at the beginning of the fall semester so that everyone would know in advance the standards by which he/she is going to be being judged. I think many people will feel that *announcing the rules at the end of the game is not a fair way to play.*

It is very significant that the professor used a **simile** when comparing the merit pay evaluation practice to giving out the grading criteria at the end of the semester: "Isn't that like a teacher passing out a syllabus with grading criteria on the last day of class?" but used a **metaphor** when comparing it to sports: "announcing the rules at the end of the game is not a fair way to play." Professors, by their profession, should be, at least equally, if not more, familiar with grading rules as with sports game rules. By opting, very likely unconsciously, for a simile for the grading comparison but a metaphor for the sports comparison, the professor assumes that all other professors see the merit pay evaluation matter as a game, betraying the fact that indeed in Americans' minds, everything in life is a sports game. In fact, another professor echoed in an ensuing message: "is this just the way the game is played?"

The statement by former Secretary of State Warren Christopher—"In the business of diplomacy, you frequently score runs . . ."—best illustrates the conflation of business, sports, and politics. Such use demonstrates Americans' total conflation of the three in comparison, revealing Americans' perception of life as sports without their own knowledge of it.[3] The reason is, to quote Lakoff and Johnson (1980),

> our conceptual system is not something we are normally aware of. In most of the little things we do every day, we simply think and act more or less automatically along certain lines. Just what these lines are is by no means obvious. One way to find out is by looking at language. Since communication is based on the same conceptual system that we use in thinking and acting, language is an important source of evidence for what that system is like. (p. 3)

Sports metaphor's ubiquity in American English strongly evidences that, in the American conceptual system, the difference between sports and business, politics, etc. is so blurred that sports have become fused with non-sport activities. I use the singular form for the word "system" to imply a collective conceptual system shared by most Americans. For any metaphor to work in any given communication, there must be a common ground--a common conceptual system shared by both the speaker and the listener.

It is no accident that Americans conflate business, politics, and sports. Again such conflation is, to a great extent, the result of the American way of life. Earlier in discussing the reasons for Americans' obsession with sport, I explained how the identity between the dominant American ideology and the perceived creeds of sport has driven people to sports. Here I would like to explore how institutionalized integration of business, politics, and sport has contributed to Americans' conceptual conflation of the three domains. As the largest capitalist country on the globe, America thrives on business--an activity through which capital is accumulated and by which American vitality is sustained. Being the world's number one democracy where everyone is encouraged, at least in ideology, to participate in governing, i.e., in politics, America witnesses politics in its grandest scale and greatest intensity. There is only one other thing in America that can compete with business and politics in terms of popularity and the extent and level of participation. That activity is none other than sport, as indicated by, among other things, the Nielsen TV ratings cited earlier. More importantly, nowhere else in the world are businesses, politics, and sports connected as closely as in America. It is well known that American sports, especially professional sports, are the product of industrialization. Yet it is less well-known that sports have, in turn, reinforced the business industry, and on a larger scale, the overall social institutions and have kept alive the American Soul--the American Dream. Business, politics, and sports constantly promote and benefit from one another.

The two types of activities that the business industry is most willing to support financially are politics and sports. Of course, businesses are not providing their support for free. Their gain in return often surpasses their contribution. While McDonalds, Coca-Cola, and many other companies compete to sponsor NBA, NFL, and other sports shows on TV, Michael Jordon and other sports stars are busy making commercials for them. The two sides are forming "joint ventures" to reap unprecedented profits. As a result, business commercials, costly as they are, flood today's sports events. The most expensive commercial rate on TV is during the Super Bowl, "$1.7 million a minute" (Weiss, 1993, p. 8). This American commercialization of sports has even invaded the Olympic Games. With millions of dollars poured in from businesses, the 1996 Atlanta Games, as NBC 's Olympics Show program anchor Bob Costas admitted at the broadcasting of the closing ceremonies, had been the most commercialized Olympic Games ever, a fact that had caused a lot of criticism and concerns throughout the world.

American businesses have grown deep into sports and have, in fact, created many sports businesses such as the NBA, NFL, and the baseball leagues. These entities are "owned" by business people and their players are "acquired" and "traded" as commodities. The business of sports has become such an important issue that the past few years alone, according to my research, witnessed, in addition to numerous articles, the publication of three books (Helyar, 1994; Gorman and Calhoun, 1994; Weiss, 1993) that are devoted exclusively to sports business. American sports, including many non-professional ones, have been totally commercialized, for "[t]he starting time of games, who plays on a team, even the existence of a big-league team in your hometown--all, in one way or another, were driven by decisions of commerce" (Gorman and Calhoun, 1994, p. 163). The comments about baseball made by Philip Wrigley, former owner of the Chicago Cubs, are especially revealing about this bizarre union between sports and business: "Baseball is too much of a sport to be a business and too much of a business to be a sport" (cited in Maikovich, 1984, p. 8).

More importantly, the already huge sports industry is growing at an alarming speed. According to Figler and Whitaker (1991, p. 177), the gross national sports product was 47.2 billion in 1986, and was projected to reach 85.4 billion this year and 121.1 billion by the year 2000. Some people may wonder what is so special about sports being business in America while the commercialization of sports has also been found in many other countries. The fact is that America is the world's leader and arguably the only superpower in this trade, setting both precedence and pace for the development of the sports industry. To see the disparity between the American sports industry and that in the rest of the world, simply look at how many top-notch players the NBA and NHL have attracted from the rest of the world by offering salaries other countries cannot afford.

In addition to business, sports are closely tied to politics. The most obvious link is, of course, the use of sports in international politics as shown in the U.S. boycott of the 1980 Moscow Olympics. Sports have also been frequently utilized to promote national pride and patriotism and, in Coakley's (1994) words, to "reaffirm the dominant political ideology of the country" (p. 366). Such use or exploitation of sports is, of course, not peculiar to America. What I want to focus on here are some unique characteristics of how sports and politics are associated in America. First, while political exploitations of sport in most countries, especially in Communist countries and countries ruled by one party which has no open rivalry, occur mostly on the international front, in America they figure prominently at local and national levels as well. It is all too common to see politicians at every level resort to sports for various political gains. For example, many city mayors consider it a great achievement to keep a ball club in the city or to lure one into the city, even at a high cost to the city and its residents.

Sports are so important a part of American life and so huge an industry that they have become politics in themselves, i.e. they are events or issues that politicians simply cannot overlook. For example, during the 1994 major baseball leagues' labor dispute, the Clinton administration intervened because, considering the importance of baseball in America, they felt that bringing the strike to an end would help build up the administration's image as an effective government which really cared about its people's concerns. Congress did not want to be left out either. Many in both Houses tried to become involved by talking about revising the labor laws specially written for the baseball leagues. The controversy arising from the strike and the events around it has further proved that baseball is not just a sports game but also a game of politics and business. Lowe (1995) demonstrates very clearly this political and business nature of baseball and other professional sports in America in his book, *The kid on the sandlot: Congress and Professional Sports 1910-1992*. Sports as politics can also be seen in the fact that it is now almost a ritual for the President to open the baseball season by throwing the first pitch and to receive in the White House the annual championship teams of the NBA, the baseball's World Series, and the college (NCAA) basketball and football programs.

Another sign of the fusion of sports and politics in America is what I call the "politicianization" of sports stars and the "sportsmanization" of politicians, a cultural model of mapping sports onto politics and vice versa. To a mind where politics and sport are conceptually blurred, the image of politicians and that of sport stars tend to merge and, as a result, it is only natural to expect sports stars to be politicians and politicians to be sportsmen. Many Americans want their sports stars to be heroes and role models. Treating sports stars as heroes and role models is not uncommon in the rest of the world, but the intensity of Americans' expectation finds no comparison. The reason for this intensity is simple: America boasts the largest media in the world which gives sports and their stars a publicity that cannot be found anywhere else. This immense publicity plus the astronomic salaries that the sports stars enjoy makes the public's expectations of them extremely high, perhaps unreasonably high (especially according to those, including some athletes, who do not believe sports stars should be role models).

The American public's embracing of sports stars as heroes is so strong that they have literally made many of them politicians, demonstrating the cultural model just mentioned. The eminent representation of professional sports players in the government at the national level provides the best proof. The current Congress boasts quite a few professional-player-turned politicians: Congressmen Jim Bunning (Kentucky), Steve Largent (Oklahoma), Jim Ryun (Kansas), and J. C. Watts (Oklahoma). Bunning was a major-league pitcher who played for the Philadelphia Phillies; Largent and Watts were both famous quarterbacks (Largent, a newly inducted Hall of Famer, played for Tulsa University in college and for the Seattle Seahawks as a professional; Watts played for the University of Oklahoma and later for the Canadian Football League). Ryun was a former world record holder in the mile run. Also worth mentioning are the recently-retired Senator Bill Bradley, a formal NBA (New York Nicks) player, and Jack Kemp, a long time politician in both the Congress and the White House administration who was equally well known for his professional football career: an AFL Most Valuable Player (1965) that twice led the Buffalo Bills to the Championship (1964-1965). Of course, Kemp is now probably better known as Bob Dole's vice president ticket in their failed bid for the White House in 1996. Yet their failure was caused primarily, as most would agree, by Dole and his strategies/policies. Finally, the wrestler Jesse Ventura beat both the Democratic and the Republican candidates to become the Governor of Minnesota. His tough sportsman image contributed greatly to his victory. Americans love competitive sports heroes! Sports stars understand well this public's political expectations of them, and many are ready to cash in, for even the "I-am-not-your-role-model" Charles Barkley is reportedly planning to run for Governor of Alabama.

The public's urge to see politicians as sportsmen is equally powerful. Driven by such an urge, today's American presidents, to use Vogler and Schwartz' (1993) words, "have felt it necessary to project a sporting image" (p. 39). All our contemporary presidents, as Figler and Whitaker (1991, pp. 274-277) illustrate, tried their best to present themselves as sportsmen. It is no wonder that former President Clinton and President Bush have followed predecessors by keeping jogging as a ritual and making fishing, golfing, and hunting their important image-boosting exercises.

As for the importance of business in America, it has already been partially shown by the enormous role of business in making sports popular as described above. A few additional points should suffice to demonstrate the enormous impact of business on American life in general. As stated earlier, perceived free competition and free enterprise form the foundation of the American way of life. From early childhood on, Americans are taught to embrace the spirit of competition, self-reliance, and entrepreneurship. This competitive entrepreneurial spirit in turn yields an enormous energy for business activities. New businesses abound daily in almost every corner of America. The fact that America has for more than half a century been the largest economy and capitalist country in the world surely speaks of the vitality and power of American business. The power of business is felt ubiquitously in America. It has invaded not only sports but also politics and many other facets of American life in a profound way. In terms of politics, the enormous amount of soft money[4] poured into the political parties and the tremendous lobby industry backed by the American corporate world wield an immense influence on the American political system. Arguably, in no other democratic capitalist country is money playing so important a role in the political process.[5] The influence of business goes beyond sports and politics. It is present in education, research, and even personal relationships and activities. In fact, everything is considered business, at least in linguistic terms: *school business, family business, and even personal business.* We *buy* and *sell* not just business products but also agendas, ideas, arguments, and sometimes ourselves as we try to *sell ourselves to potential employers.* Even "time," one of the most valuable things for mankind, is seen in monetary terms, for *time is money.* Finally, the most important thing to most Americans is *the bottom line*, given that we constantly summarize our point by stating that *the bottom line is*. . .

In summary, sports and business are arguably the most important activities in America. More importantly, they have penetrated into other aspects of American life. The integration of business, politics, and sports in American culture has certainly registered in the American mind, perhaps unconsciously, and has found its way into American English.

Notes

1. This chapter has drawn much from two of my previously published articles on the topic (Liu, 2000; Liu and Farha, 1996).

2. Communist countries also attach great importance to training young athletes, but their practice is different. In those countries, promising young athletes are taken out from regular schools and enrolled in special athletic schools. So regular schools' sports programs are truly extracurricular.

3. For a discussion of Americans' unconscious use of sports metaphor and unawareness of their perception of life as sports, please see Note 1 at the end of the Preface of the book.

4. "Soft money" refers to money donated to the political parties rather than individual candidates for advancing general political causes, but the parties involved have often used such money to promote their candidates.

5. The issue of the influence of business on American politics is a very complex one that calls for a lengthy discussion, but the topic falls outside the focus of this book. Therefore, I do not intend to and I do not think I can offer an adequate discussion of the issue. For further information on this topic, especially regarding the issue of the influence of the lobbying industry and soft money on politics, please refer to Cigler and Loomis' (1997) *Interest Group Politics*, Paul Starr's (1997) "Democracy Vs. Dollar," and Stephen J. Wayne's (2001) *Is This Any Way to Run a Democratic Election?*, especially the chapter "Has Money Corrupted Our Electoral Process?"

Chapter 3

Play Hardball and *Hit for Knockouts*: The Hard-Fought Games between the Republicans and Clinton/the Democrats

> "Some believe that a congressional hearing, like a court hearing, would be familiar *turf* for [Kenneth] Starr – easy for him to score points in."
> --Nina Totenburg, *NPR*'s Legal Affairs Correspondent, on the Republicans' decision to have Kenneth Starr as their only witness in Clinton's impeachment hearing.

> "For the past two years, we have been merely fighting downhill defense. We need to get together and start on the offense."
> --Steve Largent, Republican Congressman (Oklahoma) commenting on the Republican Party's poor performance in the 1998 congressional election

Few would probably disagree that sports metaphor is more frequently used in politics than in any other area in America. Listen to any report or discussion about politics in America and one would not fail to hear some sports jargon. In the American public discourse, sports and politics are a-married-couple-turned identical twins. Many politicians often unconsciously take politics as sports. For instance, Henry Hyde, Chairman of the Judicial Committee of the House of Representatives appeared on the October 4, 1998 Fox Network's *Fox Sunday News* to comment on the upcoming impeachment hearing concerning President Clinton. As head of the Judicial Committee, Hyde was playing a crucial role, serving as the de facto prosecutor in chief, in the impeaching process. When asked about his view about the importance of the whole issue as some questioned the motives and the necessity of the process, he immediately responded, "It's a serious game!" Then he seemed caught off guard by his own choice of words and quickly restated, "It's a serious matter." This seemingly trivial episode is of considerable significance. Of course, Hyde and his Party, who had been accused of playing a political game on this issue, would downplay what Hyde said as a slip of tongue. Yet Hyde's critics would contend that his comments clearly betrayed the fact that deep in his mind the impeachment process was nothing but a political game to embarrass or perhaps remove the President at whatever cost. Others may even go further to argue that whether Hyde's comment was an accidental speech error or not, the incident simply reveals and highlight the fact that American politics in general is a sports game. The way Americans discuss politics would certainly support this claim.

In this chapter, I will use some representative examples from the American media's coverage of the fight between the Republicans and Clinton/Democrats from 1995 to 2000 to show how politics in America is viewed as sports. As one of the purposes of the book is to introduce sports metaphors, my discussion here will not explore the use of those well-known metaphors that are hardly considered metaphorical any more such as "run a race", "running mate," "win," "beat," "play [the game] by the rules," and "game plan (political strategies)." Instead, I will focus on those that are not so well known in the rest of the world but certainly not less frequently used in the American political discourse. To help the reader better understand these metaphors, I have organized my discussion around the sports from which the metaphorical terms originate: baseball, football, and boxing.

Baseball

Baseball metaphors are very popular in politics. It has become routine for politicians to brag about *scoring runs, hitting home runs*, or forcing their opponents to *strike out* in election campaign debates, legislature battles, etc. In other words, they love playing baseball in politics, as was shown in Former Secretary of State Warren Christopher's quote in the last chapter. Politicians also like to *step up to the plate* or to *pitch*, and they sometimes enjoy *throwing curve balls*; other times they relish *playing hard ball*, as President Clinton was reported by a lot of journalists to have done during his fight with the Republicans over the budget issue in 1995. The following two quotations from two respective editorials in the January 29, 1995 issue of the *Sunday Oklahoman* each vividly illustrate how the Clinton era politics was seen as baseball games. The first, taken from Patrick B. McGuigan's editorial criticizing Clinton and his wife's behavior in the White House, reads:

> Some Democrats began to wonder, as President Bill Clinton spent his second year in office, just who was really *making his calls*. Some *in the grandstand*, and a few *on the field*, said it might be time *to bench* the man from Arkansas and *his starter*, Hillary Rodham. She's been more careful since the health care loss, but the First Spouse still wants *to pitch*, insisting that she's found her niche . . . (p. A10)

Some background information is necessary for those who are not familiar with American politics then. Unlike most first ladies before her, Hillary Clinton was allegedly heavily involved with policy issues and decision making in the White House in Clinton's early years in power, something that conservatives in America very much resented. The latter, joined by other interest groups, helped kill the health care reform plan developed by the committee that Hillary Clinton headed. The Clintons' failures and fumbles caused even some Democrats to question the First Couple's ability to lead. In McGuigan's words, the political scene in Washington was none other than a baseball game where President Clinton, his wife, and the Democratic Party leaders became players engaged in a heated debate about their game plan. To understand this editorial's message that the President and his party were in disarray, one must understand baseball and the various terms used such as "make calls," "grandstand and fields," "bench a player," and "to pitch."

The second quotation from an anonymous editorial on the same page features a baseball-defensive-play analogy: "Fiscal conservatives are one down and two to go in their drive for a balanced budget amendment" ("A Major Budget Victory," A10). It refers to the now infamous bitter fight between the Republicans and the White House over the budget that shut down the government for several days. The quote implies that attaining a budget amendment that the conservatives wanted is like winning an inning by obtaining three outs. The Republicans need just two more outs to make the amendment.

The fact that two editorials on the same page make use of baseball metaphors certainly speaks of not only baseball's high popularity but also baseball metaphors' importance in the political discourse. Whenever we opt for a metaphor, we must assume that it divulges the similarity/identity between the two things in comparison and that it renders our point clearer or more appealing to the reader. Based on this assumption, for the baseball metaphors to work in the editorial, the intended public audience must enjoy and understand baseball well, perhaps better than they do politics, and they must see the similarity/identity between the two events. More importantly, the baseball metaphors must convey the message more effectively. For most Americans, *making calls* is a far more vivid and familiar expression than "making important political decisions." So is the phrase *to pitch*. Similarly, *benching a* [political] *player* is surely livelier than "replacing a politician." Baseball metaphors are so popular in political discourse that it is no wonder when President Clinton was asked at a news conference in 1996 how he was going to deal with the Republican-controlled Congress about his deficit reduction plan, he answered that he was ready "*to play hard ball.*" To Clinton, his job was no different from a baseball player, and he surely sounded like a very proficient one! His opponents saw it the same way. After Clinton was re-elected in 1996, Senator Don Nickles, second in rank in the Republican senators, said, "The President has earned the right to *step up to the plate* and offer his program. He's going to have to *step up to the plate*" (Casteel, 1996, p. A8). Similarly, Senator Majority leader Trent Lott and House Speaker Newt Gingrich also stated, "the Present's electoral victory entitles him to the first time *at bat* next year" ("Constructive Polarization," 1996, p. A4).

A point that is worth notice with regard to the above use of baseball metaphors is that none of the speakers or writers did any explanation of the jargon since no such explanation was deemed necessary with the American public. Such is not the case when baseball metaphors are used with speakers or readers of other languages, even those who are familiar with baseball. An example in point is a July 19, 1995 (A 2) editorial written by Meng Xuan in *Shijie Ribao* (a large Taiwanese-owned Chinese newspaper in America). In the article, the author was commenting on Beijing's response to the U.S. government's allowing Taiwan's President Lee Teng-hui to visit America, and he used a baseball simile to describe Mainland China' response to Lee's visit: "If we use a baseball analogy to describe it [China's response], to America, it [China] threw a curve ball; to Taiwan, it threw a fast ball." The author then spends two lengthy paragraphs defining "curve ball" and "fast ball" and in explaining their implications. Such definition and explanation, unnecessary for the American public, were given to the Chinese readers because the latter do not have the kind of knowledge of baseball that Americans have and, more importantly, because baseball is not a well-established metaphor in Chinese culture. In other words, baseball does not play so prominent a role in the Chinese conceptual system as it does in that of Americans.

Football

Football jargon also features prominently in political discourse. Politicians are all keen about making *touch downs* in their careers. They are eager to either *quarterback* or *take the ball and run with it*. They enjoy *tackling* issues and their opponents, and they know that politics is a *four-quarter game* with the victory not decided until the *fourth quarter*. It is why Bob Dole, who was trailing behind Clinton a week before the 1996 presidential election, stood at a rally with his running mate Jack Kemp, a former NFL quarterback beside him, and told his supporters, "It's a *four quarter game*. We should keep *playing hard*, and we will *stage a great comeback victory*!"

As for politicians' love for quarterbacking, just listen to the comments that Tim Russert of NBC's *Meet the Press* made on November 3, 1998 right after the Congressional election results were known: "The surprising poor performance by the Republicans will surely cause a debate. Tomorrow, there will be a lot of *quarterbacking* within the Republican Party about why they didn't do well." The *quarterbacking* that Russert predicted soon turned into a fight and a change of leadership within the Republican Party. Such a change, in National Public Radio reporter Brian Naylor's words, was a part of football competition. On the difficult task facing Bob Livingston (who was then expected to succeed Newt Gingrich as Speaker of the House but later resigned because of an extra-marital affairs' scandal), Naylor in the November 18, 1998 NPR's *Morning Edition* program, compared it to "a football team that isn't doing as well as it once did bringing in a *new coach* after firing the old one" but as Naylor continues, "skeptics wonder if the team's glory days are behind it. For Bob Livingston the question is whether anyone can lead this team this year." Of course, Naylor was not the only one in his report who looked at the issue in football terms. When later in the report he asked former Republican House Minority Leader Robert Michel what chances the Republicans had in getting much accomplished with their slim majority (six votes margin over the Democrat) as a result of the 1998 election. Michel replied:

> When you've got a real working majority, then *you take the ball,* [and] *run with it* [meaning pushing hard their Party's agenda and legislature issues]. And even though you got a Democratic president, you enact the thing. And if he wants to veto it, well you've made your case. And if you've got enough to override, that's one thing. But in this case, boy, there'll be very slim pickings on overriding vetoes. (*NPR* "Morning Edition," November 18, 1998).

What was worse for the Republicans was, as Naylor stated, "watching from *the sidelines* are congressional Democrats who hope they can take advantage of Republican rifts to win votes on issues of importance to them." It is thus very clear from Naylor's report that the fight between the Republicans and the Democrats was an intense football contest.

The investigation and the impeachment hearing about President Clinton, as already shown in Henry Hyde's comments discussed above, were often perceived as sports games during the impeachment process. One of the sports games that the impeachment process was compared to was American football. For example, on the prospect of the appearance of Independent Counsel Kenneth Starr, a renowned attorney who appeared in many court hearings, at the House Judicial Committee's hearing, Nina Totenburg of NPR reported on the November 5, 1998 *Morning Edition* program, "Some believe that a congressional hearing, like a court hearing, would be familiar *turf* for Starr—easy for him to *score points* in." Yet because of the surprising election result where the Republicans, who had been expected to gain some seats, ended up losing a few and because the discord between the moderate and the conservative Republicans, Starr's chances of scoring points and what would happen with President Clinton were, in Totenburg's words, still unclear: "Just what is *the end game* remains in the air." In depicting Starr's familiarity with important judicial hearing processes as something in "his turf" where he "might score some points," Totenburg conveyed her idea to the American public much more vividly than she would have without using the football metaphors. Similarly, the other sports metaphor—"the *endgame* may be different"—also helped illustrate her uncertainty of Starr and the Republicans' success in the trial. Indeed, Totenburg's prediction of the endgame of this political football match turned out to be correct, for Clinton was eventually acquitted in the Senate.

In fact, as Ted Koppel of ABC's *Nightline* program put it, this game between the Republicans and Clinton was not even close because the result was determined even before the Senate hearing was over: "Like the Super Bowl last Sunday, the hoopla preceding the even was more interesting than the event itself [the Senate hearing]. These are the closing minutes of the fourth quarter of what was, after all, a lopsided game. No one doubts the outcome, but the final minutes still have to be played" ("Concluding the trial," 1999). Here, Koppel, too, used the football metaphor to depict the Clinton trial. The trial is compared to the 1999 Super Bowl in which the Denver Broncos easily beat the Atlanta Falcons 34-19 in a "lopsided game." The final part of the trial thus is equivalent to the *"closing minutes of the fourth quarter"* where even though the result of the game is already decided, the play has to continue simply for the formality of it.

Perhaps in no other speech is football so naturally woven into a political discussion as in Chris Bury's report entitled "Soft Money *Game* [italics added]" on the November 2, 1998 ABC *Nightline* program. Bury was exploring how the soft money (for the meaning of the term, see Note 2, Chapter 2) issue had impact on the election, particularly on the senate race between Democrat incumbent Senator Russ Feingold and Republican challenger Mark Newmann in Wisconsin:

> On a Sunday afternoon in Green Bay [Wisconsin], politicians know that they are hardly the *hottest tickets* in town. So yesterday before kickoff, the opposing candidates in the US Senate race *competed* for the attention of the Packer [name of the NFL team] faithful.
> ...
> The incumbent, Senator Russ Feingold, is a liberal Democrat best known for trying and failing to reform campaign finance laws with Republican John McCain. Feingold's opponent, Congressman Mark Newmann, a conservative Republican, *drafted some out of town talent to score points late in the game.* But this sporting crowd so enthusiastic about the football season seemed ambivalent at best about the *political one.*
> ...
> But by refusing Washington's money, Feingold is running a giant risk. If he's reelected, that will be touted as a popular push for campaign

finance reform. But Feingold's *defeat* will be seen as a *clumsy and stupid fumble*. Tomorrow's *contest* in Wisconsin is expected to be much closer than yesterday's game in Green Bay. This is Chris Bury for *Nightline*.

The use of football metaphors in this report makes it interesting and easy for the American public to understand. The issue at stake is, as the title of the report suggests, a *game*, a "soft money *game*." The political debates between the two parties' candidates are likened to football plays. They are said to not be the "hottest tickets" and Feingold, one of the candidates, is reported to have "*drafted some out of town talent* to score points late in the game" (referring to Hilary Clinton's appearance on Feingold's behalf). If he loses, "his defeat will be seen as *a clumsy and stupid fumble*." No lengthy and complex explanations would have more clearly expressed the reporter's ideas than the metaphors "drafted out of town talent," and "a clumsy and stupid fumble."

In a similar effective manner, Steve Largent, a Republican Congressman from Oklahoma and a former football star, revealed his disappointment at his party's poor performance in the 1998 election in his appearance on the November 8, 1998 NBC's *Meet the Press* show. He stated, "For the past two years, we have been merely fighting downhill defense. We need to get together and start on the offense." To him, his work in Congress was not much different from that in a football game he used to play and his experience in the party's poor performance was the same as in his football team's loss.

Boxing

Like baseball and football, boxing is another frequently used metaphor for politics. Politicians have often been described as engaging in boxing fights, hitting and punching each other. Sometimes they give a punch under the belt and knock out their opponents. In other words, political debate and elections are boxing matches. Listen to Stuart Rothernberg, owner and publisher of *Rothenberg Political Report*, as he explains why the Republicans did not run advertisements against Clinton by making reference to his sex scandal until a week before the 1998 election:

> We are past the early part of the impeachment process. We are past the [sic], Congress has gone out of the session now. There's a different dynamic and I think the Republicans feel that this message as the *final*

Play Hard Ball and Hit for Knockouts

STILL STANDING Clobbered with a combo—first the Starr report, then his televised testimony—Bill Clinton emerged on his feet, cut but not KO'd, and oddly, if perhaps temporarily, invigorated after absorbing his prosecutors' best shot

From *Time* magazine, October 5, 1998, p. 21

punch in the final round of the Republicans versus Democratic boxing match has some great potential... (ABC Nightline, 1998, October 28 report "The President and the election").

An even more interesting example of politics as boxing can be found in a picture in the October 5, 1998 *Time* magazine (see previous page) portraying Clinton as a wounded, but still standing boxer with his hands on the rope. The caption reads: "Still standing. *Clobbered with a combo*—first the Starr report, then his televised testimony—Bill Clinton emerged on his feet cut but not *KO'd*, and oddly, if perhaps temporarily, invigorated after *absorbing his prosecutor's best shot*." ("Still standing,"1998, p. 21). Assuming some basic knowledge of boxing on the part of the reader, this boxing metaphor, one sentence long, tersely but very vividly depicts, better perhaps than any other descriptive words or techniques, the bitter fight between President Clinton and Independent Counsel Starr. Examined closely, Starr's investigation of the Clintons was none other than a very intense, almost bloody, but also intriguing boxing match with some unexpected turns. From day one, Clinton and Starr were engaged in round after round of punches and counter punches, each side repeatedly accusing the other of foul plays such as Clinton's claims of various privileges and Starr's alleged repeated leaking of grand jury information. Again and again, they turned to the referees--the judges as well as the public--and argued for court decisions in their favor. The fight was very unpredictable. On a few occasions, Starr seemed to have lost steam, but then something would come up to revive his fight such as the Lewinsky case. Yet on a few other occasions when Starr seemed to have *KO'd* Clinton or to have him *on the ropes*, the latter came back, sometimes even stronger as the picture and its caption suggested. According to George Stephanopoulos, former Clinton aid and ABC political commentator, "Clinton may be at his best when he is *on the ropes*," meaning when he is cornered on the brink of loss. Indeed, he won in the Senate's trial, which ended in his acquittal, again by some marvelous boxing moves, to use some senators' words reported on ABC's *Nightline's* (1999, January 20) report entitled "The White House defense":

> Chris Bury (*Nightline* reporter): "It was not at all clear whether the President's lawyers had changed any minds, though several Senate Democrats proclaimed this legal *contest* all but over."

Senator John Breaux, (D), Louisiana: "I think the President's lawyers *scored both a technical knockout and a legal knockout.*"
Senator Tom Harkin, (D), Iowa: "It was an awesome one—*two punch* today on both the perjury and, the charge of perjury and the charge of obstruction of justice."
Senator Robert Torricelli, (D), New Jersey: "I suspect this day will be remembered as the beginning of the end.

It is clear that, in many politicians' minds, the impeachment process was truly a boxing match. Of course, sports metaphors used in American politics are not limited to baseball, football, and boxing. There are those from rodeo (e.g. down to the wire), golf (e.g. under par performance), fishing, and others. The most impressing point about Americans' use of sports metaphors in politics is not the great variety of sports involved but the fact that whenever it comes to political debates, Americans immediately associate them with sports because often sports metaphors appear to be the only language that could explain what is happening. The fight over the 2000 presidential election results provides perhaps the best example. The continuous recounting of the election results in Florida was history making. In describing this unprecedented process, Americans had to resort to metaphorical language. The most prominent ones used were none other than sports. The two rounds (three in some counties) of the recounting of the votes were repeatedly referred to as "overtime periods." With regard to setting up new rules of what types of votes should be counted, many Republicans yelled out "foul," claiming that rules could not be changed after the game was over. In fact, the claim framed the Republicans' major argument against the recounting. The Democrats, on the other hand, contended that the announced election results were the product of *unfair play* (i.e. voting machine and ballot problems) and *bad calls* by those in charge, such as Florida Secretary of State Catherine Harris. Hence both parties went contesting before *the referees*—the Florida State Supreme court and the Federal Supreme Court. In short, American politics is in a sense a sports game indeed.

Chapter 4

Fumbles in Wall Street and *the "Three Strikes and You're Out"* Law: The Use of Sports Metaphors in Other Areas of American Life

> "And with our usual warning that even all-stars like these [financial experts] can occasionally, dare I say it, *strike out*, let's ask these sluggers to try to *hit some second- half home runs* . . ."
> — Louis Rukeyser of *PBS*' *Wall$treet with Louis Rukeyser*

In addition to politics, Americans also relish viewing many other aspects of life as sports, including business, education, law, and personal life. Let us first look at how business activities are constantly referred to as sports. Day in and day out, no matter what business it is, be it sales, service, or manufacturing, people are engaged in a continuous competition trying to *beat their competitors* or to *score a home run* or even a *slam dunk* in a *deal*. We are constantly reminded that business is a game because "in business, the bottom line is *the name of the game.*" The hallmark of the business world, the stock market, is also a sports arena where *bull and bear runs* alternate. So everything in business, from marketing to sales to investment, is a sports game to play and win. Many business people literally merge the two in their practice and mentality.

Take for instance the advertisement flier (next page) made by a real estate agent. The flier features a heading slogan which reads "Going out

GOING TO BAT FOR OUR CLIENTS

Expect the best

PLANNING TO SELL YOUR HOME OR INVESTMENT PROPERTY ?
I NEED YOUR HELP. . .to locate the properties that will be coming up for sale in our neighborhood in the next sixty (60) days.

CALL TODAY...!!!...FOR YOUR FREE!!!!
COMPETITIVE MARKET ANALYSIS COMPARABLE SALES IN THE AREA

YOU ARE INVITED TO CALL ANYTIME WITH YOUR REAL ESTATE QUESTIONS.

FACTORS THAT MOST INFLUENCE THE SALE OF YOUR PROPERTY
1. Price
2. Condition of Property
3. Location of Property
4. Terms Offered

Expect the best ®

MULTI-MILLION $$ PRODUCER

to bat for our clients" and a drawing of a baseball player batting on a realtor's house sale sign. It implies that the agent will try to help his clients to sell their houses as a baseball player would bat for homeruns. The most striking thing in his flier is the way sports and business are merged literally and figuratively both in words and picture. In the slogan "Going out to bat for our clients," the sports jargon "bat" and the business term "clients" literally marry the two professions. The marriage is further reinforced by the picture in the flier: a baseball player batting on top of a realtor's sales sign with the word "sold" on it, and under the sales sign a picture of the "multi-million $ producer" agent (the picture as well as the name of the agent has been deleted to protect the agent's identity). The picture signifies a convergence of the agent and the baseball player over the sales sign: the player stands for the agent and the agent becomes the player. For a flier like this to work, the realtor agent assumes the public's knowledge of baseball and their appreciation of the similarities between baseball and the realty business and between sports and business in general.

Sports jargon also figures prominently in high-brow business professionals' speeches in very formal contexts. Louis Rukeyser, a renowned financial expert, provides a really good example of business professionals' love for sports jargon. Regular viewers of the "Wall Street Week with Louis Rukeyser" must have been impressed with Rukeyser's sports knowledge and his habitual vivid and effective use of sports jargon. In his commentary, successful investors have often been said to have *made a touch down* and *danced in the end zone*, while other investors have either *struck out* or *waited on the side line*. Even when inviting his guests to make investment recommendations on his show, he does it in sports terms: "And now with our usual warning that even *all-stars* like these can occasionally *strike out*, let's ask these *sluggers* to try to *hit some second-half home runs* for us by revealing the specific investments they are now recommending for the rest of 1995" (June 30, 1995). Similarly, he ties Wall Street naturally with sports, particularly football, in his opening remarks on the January 29, 1999 show, for the whole speech was threaded together with football and some other sports plays.

>Good evening. I'm Louis Rukeyser. This is Wall Street Week. Welcome back.
>Well, it's the weekend of the Super bowl but it's going to be tough for either team *to score more touchdowns* than the super-charged stock market has racked up in January.

Roaring back, as has become customary, from its mid-month pause, which had briefly, and predictably, *brought the media bears out of hibernation* again, Wall Street turned in *an all pro performance* that surmounted all the *crazy stadium noise* that was reverberating from Washington to Rio. . . .

Are you a believer yet? This week, even the constitutionally cautious Federal Reserve Chairman Alan Greenspan, who gets paid to be cranky about such things, allowed how, while *picking the winners* among many of the Internet stocks was akin to buying a lottery ticket, so fundamental were the economic changes now afoot that the frenzy about the overall industry was, in his works, "potentially sound."

. . . with a stronger-than-expected 5.6 percent rate of growth in the final quarter of 1998, the most vigorous consumer spending in 14 years and the least inflation in 40 years, every major stock index gathered strength and made it a *winning* month.

I hate to irritate athletes as tough as *the Denver Broncos and the Atlanta Falcons,* but this may be the year we don't really care about the *Super Bowl indicator.*

After all, Wall Street defied tradition last year by *putting the bears to rout* once again, even after the *Super Bowl victory* of the Broncos, who were not an original National Football League team, and therefore presumably a jinx for investors. . . .

Wall Street's attitude these days seems to be: Let the chips fall where they may, as long as they're microchips.

In Washington, to be sure, the effort *to bench* the President was continuing with the possibility of a lively few minutes of guest commentary from *rookie* Monica Lewinsky.

In Rio de Janeiro, it would have taken a particularly *speedy wide receiver to catch the Brazilian reel,* as it headed earthward for the eighth straight day. . .

Even *Coach Greenspan* was expressing awe and bewilderment. Recalling his own prediction that the U.S. could not remain "an oasis" in a troubled world, he admitted that "so far, we've managed to do that" and, furthermore, that "there's no evidence that that is about to change."

This, from the fellow whose *defensive game plan* used to be headed "irrational exuberance."

Now apparently, he thinks it's all suddenly become surprisingly rational.

Has it? Or is a euphoria that now seems to have spread even to professionally dour central bankers a sign, at last, that *a major interception is lurking just down the field?*

We'll explore that tonight with our all-knowing panelists . . . .But, first, let's check *the fumbles* on Wall Street.

In Rukeyser's description, conducting business on Wall Street is thus playing football. Traders and the businesses are trying to score touchdowns, receive a particularly speedy pass, avoid interceptions and fumbles, design good defensive plans, etc. Federal Reserve Chairman Allen Greenspan was thus called "Coach Greenspan." Even President Clinton and the infamous White House Intern Monica Lewinsky became football players in his discussion with Clinton being referred to as a could-be-benched player and Lewinsky as a rookie player. Listeners who had little knowledge of American football surely would have found quite a few terms and expressions in this short speech of Rueyser's quite puzzling such as "*a major interception is lurking just down the field.*"

Other business journalists also often report business activities in sports jargon. In his report entitled "Week of Reckoning for Earnings," Eric Wahlgren, a Reuters business reporter, began this way: "With more *heavyhitters stepping up to the plate* this week to report earnings than in any other week in the quarter, investors will want to see a lot of *home runs* before socking more money into stocks." (1999). Stock market activities and baseball play merged seamlessly in his report. Big companies scheduled to report their earnings have become star baseball players getting ready to play, and good earnings have been compared to home runs. As another example, in a *Business Week* article about Singapore's chances of becoming a major financial player, Barnathan (1995, p. 55) writes, "some analysts question whether Singapore's tight control on information will hinder its efforts to join *the big leagues.*" In this statement, baseball metaphor is applied to international business. Countries are compared to American baseball teams that are grouped into tiers (big leagues and small leagues) according to their strengths. When banks were allowed to engage in insurance businesses, it was reported by various media as being allowed to *play on the other's turf*, a football term.

A report entitled "Women Executives Find It Pays to Speak Sports" carried in the *Daily Oklahoman* further evidences the importance of sports metaphors in business:

> It's the 18th hole and you've got to roll in a slippery 50 foot side hill putt to land the biggest contract of your corporate career. As the seconds tick down, you know you have to complete that Hail Mary pass if you're going to get that signature on the dotted line.
> Excuse me?

For the sports impaired, life in the corporate world always has been tough. High-level executives strike deals on the golf course. Corporate memos are riddled with lingo only a devoted sports fan could interpret.
There's one thing the ambitious up-and-comer can do.
Learn how to speak sports.
So around the country, people are turning to clinics where they learn the lingo.
"Historically, men have been able to mix the pleasure of golf with the purpose of business," said marketing executive Barbara Simpson, 45. "That is an option that should be readily available to women."
She took a $30, one day, women-only "Golf Networking" course from Peter Titlebaum, Professor of health and sports science at the University of Oklahoma. . . .
Titlebaum's sessions are limited to women because, he said, *women executives risk losing business if they don't "speak sports."* "Men are going to continue to talk this language of sports, regardless," Titlebaum said. "So women can either choose to play this or not." ("Women Executives," 1997, p. C3).

The statement that "women executives risk losing business if they don't 'speak sports'" might be somewhat hyperbolic, but it surely highlights the importance of sports knowledge and sports language in American business. In fact, some common American business terms have come from sports such as a *good/bad deal, ballpark figure, rain check*, to name just a few. The word *deal*, a term borrowed from poker games, has been used to refer to any kind of business transactions. The term *ballpark figure* means an estimated number, and it came from baseball. In the early days of baseball, it was a common practice to give an estimate when reporting the number of people that attended a game. The term *rain check* also originated from an old practice in baseball. Baseball teams give spectators a rain check when they allow them a free second visit to a game that has been rained out and re-scheduled. Many businesses today write their customers rain checks to guarantee them a product with the same price when it is temporarily out of stock.

Sports metaphor is also often employed in education in America. As explained in Chapter Two, it is a very-well known fact that students and schools are competing fiercely in sports, an activity that occupies a very prominent place in American schools. Schools, of course, also compete for other things such as academic reputation, grants, etc., but such competition is frequently secondary to those in sports. As pointed out in Chapter 2, the comment that an official from the Santa Fe High

School in Edmond, Oklahoma, made after her school won a state academic bowl in 1998 best supports this point: "Winning a competition like this, Crittendon said, is like winning a state championship in football" (Hartman, 1998, p. A9). The dominance of sports competition cannot be better expressed. That is why achievement in academia in American sometimes has to be portrayed in sports' terms in order to be more accessible and clearer to the general public. That is exactly what Bobby Ross Jr. (1997, June 23) did in a newspaper article in *the Daily Oklahoman* describing a high school student's effort to attain the highest score on ACT in order to win scholarships to go to college. Ross Jr. renders his discussion completely in baseball terms, and very effectively:

> Some high school students *hit a home run* every time they *step to the plate*—the academic plate, that is.
> Steven Purdy *bats cleanup* on that Triple R--reading, 'riting, and 'rithmetic--team.
> As a Classen School of Advanced Studies junior, the 17-year-old scored a composite 35 out of a possible 36 on the ACT. On the SAT, the Oklahoma City student made a perfect 800 on the mathematical portion and a 690 on the verbal.
> Purdy's scores on both major college entrance exams place him in the upper echelon of students nationwide--and practically guarantee him admission to any college or university.
> Bu Purdy--not satisfied with anything short of *a grand slam*--plans to take both tests again. . .
> So goes the *fast-pitch* competition for lucrative scholarships, prestigious university admission—and, perhaps, most importantly, academic bragging rights.
> In this *extra-inning* examination, every penciled-in A, B C or D counts.
> . . .
> "With that [the 35 ACT score]," he [a school counselor] said, "they'[schools] ll almost buy you a car to go to school. *It's kind of like being 7-2 and being able to play basketball.*" (*The Daily Oklahoman, The Oklahoma City Times pages,* pp. 1, 3)

In this report, taking college admission tests is compared to batting in baseball, scoring a very high score to hitting a home run, and obtaining a full score to a grand slam. The fact that Ross employs baseball metaphor to discuss a topic on education is very significant. As I stated earlier, whenever we opt for a metaphor in our communication, we must believe that the metaphor divulges the similarity between the two things in comparison and will make our point clearer or more appealing to the reader. Therefore, the general public must know baseball better than college admission tests, and the baseball metaphor will hence enable the reader to more appreciate the competitiveness of college admission examinations. The comparison of scoring 35 to being 7-2 playing basket ball assumes that the American public are more familiar with the latter phenomenon than the former, and such an analogy will make the scarcity of a 35 ACT score clearer and easier to understand.

Sports metaphor has also invaded many other aspects of American life. A few examples should suffice to illustrate the point. In law, prosecutors and defendant lawyers are constantly referred to in reports as players on opposing teams trying to score points and defeat each other in the court. They are said to have scored a "knock-out punch," "win a game in a series," "fumbled," etc. Numerous instances of such use can be found in the media's coverage of the O.J. Simpson case. For one, Jack Ford (1995), NBC's chief legal correspondent for the case, when asked on the *Today Show* to comment on the Simpson trial prosecutors' attitude towards the defense team's upcoming presentation of their case in the court, said (in the prosecutor's voice) "Now is your time to *step up to the plate* and let's see what you can do." Here, to present a legal case is compared to playing baseball—"step up to the plate," a place where the batter is to swing the bat to hit the ball thrown at him in order to score points. Ford's reference was that thus far, the prosecution had remained in an offensive posture and had run into some problems. Now it was the defense team's turn to substantiate their claims. The prosecutors were suspicious that Simpson's attorneys could accomplish theirs when *they step up to the plate* attempting to score points. Of course, the best-known example of sports metaphors in law is perhaps the "Three strikes and you're out" law used in several states to severely punish (life time imprisonment) criminals with repeated offences. "Three strikes and you're out" is a baseball rule of play: if a player swings the bat without contacting three times, then the batter is out. Borrowing this concept, legislators made it a law to imprison for life those offenders who committed violent crimes three times.

Sports metaphors are ubiquitous in Americans' daily life, too. Americans like to "touch base" with their friends and colleagues, and want to "cover all the bases" in what they do. When someone does not "play by the rules" in a work place, they call it "foul play." When someone does things irrationally, the person is said to be "out in left field.' When one fails to accomplish something, it is called a "strike out." When one is being deceitful, the person is considered to be "throwing a curve ball." When colleagues sit together informally to discuss issues and make decisions, they are said to "get in a huddle," a practice that football, basketball, and other sports players in a team often conduct to decide and communicate the chosen play to be implemented. Even very intimate personal relationships are often seen in sports terms. For example, many youths use the baseball jargon "got to the first base" with a girlfriend to mean "had a kiss" or "had a good beginning of a intimate relationship," and the phrase "hit a home run" with a date to imply having "slept with" the person. In an article discussing the life of Freddie Prinze, Jr., a rising movie star, Dotson Rader, the author, gives the following caption to one of the pictures of Prinze to highlight what Prinze is trying to accomplish: "Prinze tries to *make it to the Major Leagues*—and *to first base with* Jessica Biel" (Rader, 2001, p.5). In this caption, super stardom becomes Major Leagues and falling in love turning into "getting to the first base." Another interesting sports metaphor used to describe a personal relationship can be found in a comment that Jerry Seinfeld, the protagonist in the well-known situation-comedy *Seinfeld*, made regarding Kelly's (a female character) sudden change of mind about dating the character George: "there is always the possibility that she called an audible. . . . she got up to the line of scrimmage, didn't like the looks of the defense, and changed the play" (1994, p. 20). It is a rather common practice in football play that after both the offense and defense sides are lined up, the quarterback looks at the defense and changes the original offensive play. It is called an "audible." Here in the comedy, dealing with personal relationship becomes football play, a rather vivid description that requires, though, good football knowledge on the part of the viewers.

Sports metaphors have even found their way into medicine in America. According to the article "Is sports jargon pure jibberish?: Just plain English, please!" (1995, p. C8), quite a few terms for medical conditions also came from sports injuries. For example, *hip pointer* (bruising of the area on one's waist area) and *turf toe* (painful condition caused by the hypertension and subsequent inflammation of the toe joint) both developed from injuries from playing football with the latter appearing after the use of artificial turf in football. *Cauliflower ear* (an injured ear with build-up of blood adjacent to the cartilage within the ear) originated with wrestling. These examples surely further corroborate the ubiquitousness of sports metaphor in American English.

Chapter 5

Buying an Argument and *Selling an Agenda* in *Retail Politics*: Business Metaphors in American English

"My job [as the Chair of the Republicans in the House] is to *sell* to the public our Party's messages..."
    --J. C. Watts, Congressman (Oklahoma) speaking of his duties as the new Republican Conference Chair in the House, November 22, 1998

"A candid dialogue with China could *yield dividends* [in the long run]."
    --Madeleine Albright, former U.S. Secretary of State, commenting on her visit to Beijing, March 2, 1999

Business metaphors also figure very prominently in American discourse. Although they are not as numerous as sports metaphors, business metaphors are extensively used in American English and, more importantly, like sports metaphors, they occur frequently in daily conversations and serve to betray some of the fundamental views of life and the world that Americans hold. The most basic but convincing piece of evidence is the broad use of the word "business." We constantly hear the expression "taking care of business," and most of the time it does not refer to financial/business dealings but to daily chores. When Americans say they have some "business" to take care of, they really mean things like taking their children to school, having their car serviced, or going to the doctor. Of course, Americans may argue that these are indeed "personal businesses." Yet such use of the word "business" is not allowed in Chinese or many other languages. For example, the expression "I've some business to take care of" has to be translated into "I've some *things* to take care of" in Chinese because the word "business" ("shenyi" in Chinese) is limited to financial or trade dealings only. In other words, Chinese make a very clear distinction between business and non-business activities. Americans, on the other hand, do not, at least not in language use. Instead, Americans tend to conflate business with many other matters.

Let us first look at how Americans view politics in business terms. One example can be found in the comments that Congressman J.C Watts of Oklahoma made on *Flashpoints*, a political TV show in Oklahoma, on November 22, 1998 after he was elected Chair of the Republican Conference in the House of Representatives. Asked by the host of the show to explain what he planned to do in the new leadership position, Watts stated, "My job is to *sell* to the public our Party's messages." Then when requested to answer what had led to the shakeup of the Republican leadership in the House, he said, "As a result of the election, our Party's *market share* in the House had decreased. We had to look our organization *from the CEO to the janitor* to see what necessary changes had to be made." His entire comment here was based on business metaphors. Convincing the public about his Party's ideas and policies has become the business of "selling." The number of House seats occupied by Republicans is rendered as "market share." The Republican group in the House has been compared to a business structure with its leading members (the speaker and the Party "whip") as "CEOs" at the top and the non-ranking members and secretaries as "janitors" at the bottom.

Another interesting example of business metaphors in political discourse can be found in the October 28, 1998 *Nightline* report, entitled "The President and the Election," on the impact President Clinton's scandal had on the election of the House of Representatives. In one section, the report was about the race in Ohio's Sixth Congressional District between the Democratic candidate Representative Ted Strickland and the Republican candidate Lt. Governor Nancy Hollister. Because of the Republican Party's fundraising advantage, Hollister's campaign was much better funded than Strickland's and ran many more advertisements, too. As a result,

Strickland had to rely more on going out to the public in person. Here is the section from the *Nightline* report:

> Jonathan Riskind (from *The Columbus Dispatch* paper): Strickland, basically, I think, has worked for two years to do the kind of *retail politics* that will help you in that district, but it's a huge district. You can't shake everybody's hand.
> Michel McQueen (*Nightline* reporter): Not that Strickland and Hillister aren't trying. (Interviewing Hollister) A lot people are talking about the importance of the get-out-the-vote effort.
> Lt. Gov. Nancy Hollister: Right.
> Michel McQueen: Are you making any extraordinary efforts to get people to come out?
> Lt. Gov. Nancy Hollister: Absolutely. *The bottom line* in this election is going to be how many folks you get to the polls.
> Michel McQueen: If the Hollister campaign is *counting on* an edge from its advertising, Strickland is *banking on* help from a big name [meaning Mrs. Clinton]. (Italic emphasis added)

Four business metaphors, *retail politics*, *bottom line*, *count on*, and *bank on*, were used by three different people in this short episode of the report. In their mind, politics was business. Hence there is *retail politics*, which is in contrast with *wholesale politics*. Like retail business, *retail politics* operates on a much smaller scale than *wholesale politics*. In the former, you promote candidacy, your political views, policies, etc. by approaching the voters and the public one by one or group by group, but in the latter, you sell your views and policies on a much larger scale through big TV advertisements on major network. That is why what counts in politics was subsequently compared to *the bottom line* on an accounting sheet: either you win (showing profit on the bottom line) or you lose (showing loss on your bottom line).

Since politics is business, one thus needs to *count* or *bank on* others for help, i.e. getting assistance, often financially. In fact, a politician, or any person for that matter, who can be of help to someone or some organization is called a *credit* or an *asset*. An individual who is of negative impact is a *liability*. It is no wonder that, during the Clinton presidency, political pundits were constantly debating whether Mrs. Clinton was an asset or a liability to Mr. Clinton. Similarly, the same experts were wondering if Mr. Clinton was an asset or liability to Mrs. Clinton during her run for the Senate seat. Furthermore, the results of political moves are also often viewed in monetary terms. For example, commenting on her meetings with Chinese leaders in her March, 1999, visit to China, Secretary of State Madeleine Albright stated that her "candid dialogue" with the Chinese was very meaningful and *"could yield dividends"* ("Albright: No apologies," 1999). In this speech, political maneuvers were simply business strategies to gain dividends. Politics as business and sports is perhaps most tersely highlighted in the headline and the lead sentence of Reuters' David Wiessler's report after the 1998 election. The headline reads "Democrats Back *in Business* After U.S. Elections" and the lead reads "Democrats declared Wednesday that their odds-defying election victories showed they were back *in the political ballgame* and Americans wanted to shut off talk of impeaching President Clinton" (Wiessler, 1998). Politics is both business and sports in Wiessler's words.

Like sports metaphors, business metaphors are not limited to politics in America. They have found their way into every other facet of American life, law, education, and everyday personal business. In law, for example, during a discussion of the value of Michael Fortier in the prosecutor's case against the Oklahoma City Federal building bombing suspect Timothy McVeigh on the May 13, 1997 *The News Hour with Jim Lehrer*, Tim Sullivan, a commentator, said, "Fortier was the government's *high billing*. Now the question is whether he *lived up to his billing.*" Here the government's heavy reliance on Fortier in building its case against McVeigh was presented in terms of investment in public promotion of a product. Sullivan was questioning whether it was a worthwhile investment on the part of the government to use Fortier in the case. Business metaphors also function in the discussion of education. In an editorial in the May 9, 1997 *Daily Oklahoman*, Walter Williams (1997, p. A.4) criticizes some of the Oklahoma educators' new ideas and their effort to implement them, claiming, "Nowhere are half-witted education ideas given *greater currency."* In Williams's words, to believe in some education ideas is tantamount to paying for and buying some conceptual products. Williams was not alone in seeing education matters in monetary terms. In arguing for "school choice" for parents and in refuting the idea that "school choice" would take money away from public schools, Thomas Sowell (1999, p. A. 5) wrote: "Perhaps only a generation that has already suffered from dumbed-down education would *buy* the half-baked argument about 'draining money from the public schools.'" Like politics, education is also for sale.

Business metaphors are even more common in Americans' daily life. Almost anything is perceived as money. For example, "Time is money"; therefore to use one's time wisely and efficiently, one has to *budget one's time*, an expression that cannot be translated directly or literally into Chinese where an equivalent expression is "to plan using one's time." Ideas are also money as Steen and Gibbs (1999) show. Examples include "Let me put my *two cents' worth*. He is *rich* in ideas. That book is a *treasure trove* of ideas. He has a *wealth* of ideas" (Steen and Gibbs, 1999, p. 1). There are of course many other money metaphors such as "be right on the money" (meaning being accurate and to the point), and "money talks." Additional examples in this group include *cash in* (to take advantage of a situation), a *million-dollar question* (the most important question), *feel like a million dollars* (feel very good), *put one's money where one's mouth is* (to mean what one says and keep one's word), *put in one's two cents worth* (to give one's opinion), and *pass the buck* (evade one's responsibility by giving it to others). Similarly, in monetary terms, as stated earlier, a positive personal trait or a useful person is an *asset* or *credit*, a negative trait or person is called a *liability*, and a person not trustworthy is termed one that has *no credit*. To appreciate a person's effort or contribution in a matter is to *give credit* to that person. Not to give that person the due credit is to *sell that person short*. In fact, one can "buy" and "sell" almost anything in American English. One can *buy* an argument, *buy* time (to gain some time when one is behind a schedule on something or one is trailing in a context, etc), *buy* a good review (to receive a good review such as "This movie could not buy a good review at all"), etc. Conversely, one can *sell* an idea, a stand/position on an issue, a policy, or even oneself (meaning to market oneself for a job). One can *buy* into an argument or have an idea *sold* to him/her. Besides these obvious business metaphors, there are many less obvious ones, too, which do not involve the words "money," "cash," "buy," or "sell."

For instance, in discussing a move that is difficult and challenging at the moment but will be beneficial in the long run, Americans like to consider it a decision that will eventually *pay off*. It is therefore common to hear them say it *pays off* or *doesn't pay off* to do something. Viewing things in monetary terms, Americans have also made the phrase *the bottom line* an extremely popular one. Anything that is the most important to consider in a decision is *the bottom line*, and they have turned it into almost a ritual to conclude their remarks with the statement beginning with "*the bottom line* is . . If people have asked for and have been given things that they cannot handle, they are believed to have *got more than they bargained for*. Along the same line, they like to use or turn their strengths or advantages into good *bargaining chips* (leverages) in their dealing with others. If they make a mistake, they often have to *pay the price*, but sometimes even if they made a serious mistake that has severe consequences, they may still be *bailed out* (be saved) by others or by their own smart moves. Everything *has a price* (not free or involving work and effort). Of course, even when they work hard to earn what they deserve, they sometimes may get *short changed* (cheated) by others in whatever ventures they are engaged in. When that happens and the two parties become involved in a dispute, they will be urged to look at the issue *from the other side of the coin*, meaning from the other point of view or a different perspective. Furthermore, a secondary and often unintended or unexpected result of an action is called a *byproduct*, again a business concept in loan. In summary, American life in essence is often business indeed.

Chapter 6

"Dangjia" [*Managing family*] and *"Chiku"* [*Eating Bitterness*] at Work: Family and Eating in Chinese Culture and Language

> "A very important goal of the economic reform is to stop the practice of *chi daguo fan* [*eating from the big rice pot,* meaning relying on the government] and to *da po tie fanwan* [*break the iron rice bowl,* meaning to eliminate life-time job security]."
>
> "*Dangjia zuozhu de laodong renmin* [the working people who *manage the family* and who are the masters] have to produce more profit for the country and to increase the state's revenues. . ."
>
> —Deng Xiaoping, late Chinese leader and the architect of the economic reform in China

To appreciate the importance of family in Chinese culture and the unique prominence of the family metaphor in the Chinese language, one needs to go no further than looking at the Chinese term *guojia*, which translates into English as "country" or "state." Like many words in Chinese, it is a compound noun consisting of two individual characters: "guo" (meaning "state") and "jia" (meaning "family). So in Chinese, a country is a "state-family." If a state is viewed as a family, many things and practices will be understandably seen in the same light. The state is thus frequently referred to as *gongjia* ["public family"] and anything that belongs to the state is *gongjia de* ["the public family's"]. Similarly, to lead or be in charge of a government, or any institution for that matter, is to *dang jia* ("managing [the] family"). Government officials are often referred to as *fumu guan* ("father-mother officials"). Although the number of family metaphors used in the Chinese language is not enormous, especially in comparison with that of eating metaphors, family metaphors are important in Chinese because, as the above few examples illustrate, they reveal how the Chinese view some of the fundamental structures of society and some basic issues of life. While it is not difficult to appreciate the importance of family in Chinese culture, it is even easier to understand the unusual significance of eating therein, for the most common expression of greeting among friends and colleagues in Chinese is "Have you eaten?" and eating metaphors are almost ubiquitous in the Chinese language. *Chi baizan* ("eat a defeat"), *chi guansi* ("eat a lawsuit"), *chi jing* ("eat a surprise" meaning being shocked), *chi qui* ("eat a loss" meaning suffer a loss in a unfair way), *chi xiang* ("eat fragrance" meaning being popular or being able to have one's own way) are just a few examples of the numerous eating metaphors in the Chinese language. Basically, one can eat almost anything in the Chinese language as can been seen in the list of the popular eating metaphors in the Glossary of Dominant Metaphorical Idioms at the end of the book. Why are "family" and "eating" so important in the Chinese consciousness? A brief review of Chinese history and a close examination of some Chinese customs will shed some light.

The role and importance of family in Chinese culture

The term *guojia* or "state-family" is a good starting point to learn of the tremendous and unusual role that family has played in shaping the Chinese political system, business practice, and other aspects of life.[1] "Unlike individual-centered Western culture, Chinese culture revolves around the family," and in this family-dominant culture, "the whole country is a big family where the emperor is the number-one head" (Wang Lixiong, 1998, p. 26). For thousands of years, "China, has been a *jiaguo jeside zongfa shehui* [a patriarchal tribe-like society where the family and the Sate are interwoven]" (Feng Tianyu and Zhou jiming, 1989, p. 41). It is no wonder Mo Zi (also known as Mo Tsu), a famous

Chinese philosopher (431-397 BC), stated, "Ruling countries everywhere in the world is the same as ruling a family" (Mo Zi's *Part Two of Shan Tong*). The fundamental structure of the traditional Chinese society is defined explicitly as *junjunchengcheng, fufuzizi* [the emperor and his subjects; the father and sons]. In such a system, state affairs are conducted like family business. The head of the government rules the country the way a father of a family rears his children. In fact, government officials are treated like parents. The Chinese names for chief government officials such as *shengzhang* [governor], *xianzhang* [county governor] and *shizhang* [mayor] all contain the character *zhang*, which means "senior." In fact, historically, as shown in Chinese *Ci Yuan* (*Etymology of words)*, many government official titles contained the word *jia* [family] such as *jiachen, jiali,* and *jiajun* ("Jia," 1988, p. 453). Hence, citizens often refer to these officials as *fumu guan* [father-mother-officials], a title that officials enjoy using for self-reference because they like to pledge to live up to their duties as such. The concept of rulers and officials being parents was pushed to the extreme during the Cultural Revolution (1966-1976) in China. A popular "revolutionary song" in that era demonstrates this clearly. The second line of the song reads "Father is dear and Mother is dear but they are not as dear as Chairman Mao." So stated, the ruler is clearly viewed as the ultimate true father of the citizens. By the same analogy, Chinese people are often called *zhonghua ernu* [sons and daughters of China] by both the rulers and the citizens themselves.

If the whole society, including its political and economic system, is treated as a family, it then follows that harmony rather than competition, which often leads to contention and dispute, is emphasized Of course, it does not mean that competition does not exist or is not allowed in China. It only implies that it is not a priority in a family-oriented culture, and it is surely not as valued as it is in a culture where competition forms the foundation of its culture like in America. The traditional Chinese family is one with multiple generations living under one roof ruled by the oldest male, the patriarch. Such a family structure is still intact in some rural areas in China. In such a family, the patriarch rules by authority. Everyone should obey his order. Every member of the family works for the family and whatever is produced will be distributed--supposedly evenly--by the patriarch. This concept or archetype of "family" is still deeply rooted in the Chinese psyche today. Since the founding of the People's Republic of China in 1949, the Beijing government and its leaders have both explicitly and implicitly assumed the role of the patriarchs and have even divided its citizens by trade in family terms. Factory workers are called *gongren laodage* [worker senior-big brothers]; peasants are *nongmin bobo* [farmer senior uncles], and the People's Liberation Army soldiers are *jiefanjun shushu* [Liberation Army uncles]. Beijing even extended the family metaphor to portray its relationships with other communist countries. Back in the 1950s when Moscow and Beijing enjoyed very close ties, Beijing was always bragging about the Big Socialist Family [the Socialist camp] and called the Soviet Union "Senior Big Brother." Although these specific terms have long disappeared from the Chinese political discourse, the practice is still alive today, for as recently as September 2, 2001, Chinese Foreign Minister Tang Jiaxuian, in commenting on Chinese President and Communist Party Secretary General Jiang Zemin's visit to North Korea, China's Communist neighbor and ally, said that Jiang's trip "was a visit to a relative. Unlike what happens in a typical head of state visit to another country, the ceremonies and procedures for this trip are casual . . ." ("Jiang Zemin fang chaoxian: zou qinqi [Jiang Zemin's trip to North Korea: A visit to a relative]," 2001).

Of course, weaving a family tree among its citizens is nothing new and surely not the patent of the current Beijing government. Indeed, the use of family titles with non-family members has been a common traditional practice in China. Historically, residents of a village have used family address forms to promote loyalty and harmony in their community even though they often have no blood relationship. Members of the younger generation are taught to address those of their parents' generation using the title "uncle or aunt." The typical address form is last name plus the person's age rank among those in his/her generation plus the tile uncle or aunt, such as "Wang second Uncle" and "Li third Aunt." Similarly, the young have to address members of their grandparents' generation using the title "Grandpa X" or "Grandma X." Such practice is still common even in the cities where children are supposed to address their parents' colleagues and friends "uncles" or "aunts." It has been a long tradition for apprentices or young workers in a factory or company to address their immediate supervisor or the person who mentors or trains them *shifu* ("master") and the person's wife *shimu* ("master mother"). It has been and still is a popular practice in Taiwan for students in a school to address class or school mates by *xuezhang* (school older brother), *xuedi* (school younger brother), *xuejie* (school older sister), or *xuemei* (school younger sister). Although such practice can also be found in America, it is mostly limited to fraternities and sororities, not the school at large.

One unique feature about the Chinese family structure in terms of address forms is its rigid hierarchy not only across generations but also within the same generation, a feature that helps maintain family order and harmony. For example, the age difference, and hence the rank, of the brothers and sisters are distinguished in the address forms. Brothers who are older are called "*xiong*" formally and "*ge*" informally whereas the word for younger brothers is "*di*." The sisters older than you are "*jie*" whereas the sisters younger than you are "*mei*." So every time you introduce a brother or sister of yours, the words will automatically indicate whether he/she is older or younger than you, unlike in English where you usually do not distinguish them and when you do, you have to add the words "elder" or "younger." The same distinction is made with uncles and aunts in Chinese. The word for uncles older than your father is "*bofu*" whereas the word for uncles younger than your father is "*shu*." The rigidity of the family hierarchy can also be seen in the practice in which older siblings address their younger ones by the latter's first name but the younger siblings have to address the older ones by using the words "*ge*" for a brother and "*jie*" for a sister. This clear hierarchy helps assign every family member to the "right place" in the family structure, discouraging competition and ensuring easy and smooth governing in the family. When such rigid hierarchical structure is extended to social institutions as it has often been the case as shown in titles like *Uncle Second Li* and *School Older Brother* mentioned above, it helps to maintain the patriarchal governing system in the society. It is no wonder that Beijing's rulers, who view themselves as family heads both synchronically and diachronically, have frequently used the genealogical term X *dai* [X generation] to refer to each of the successive leaderships in the history of People's Republic of China. For example, Deng Xiaoping on many occasions stated that Mao Zedong was the head of the first generation of the Beijing government, Deng himself the second generation, and Jiang Zemin the third generation (Deng Xiaoping, 1993, Vol. 3, pp. 298-299, 380-381). He called Mao as well as Marx and Lenin "*lao zuzong*" ["old ancestors"], claiming the Beijing leadership "could not forsake its *lao zuzong*" (Deng Xiaoping, Vol. 3, p. 369). While it is significant that such genealogical references to the Communist leaders are wide-spread in Chinese media and in the documents of the government, it is even more noteworthy that the hierarchy of this leadership genealogy has been strictly maintained as it would in a traditional Chinese family. As a rule, the members of the older generation of the leadership, even after their retirement, often have a significant and even decisive say in important government issues. For instance, it is a well-know fact that Deng Xiaoping and his retired octogenarian colleagues played a crucial role in the June 4, 1989 Tiananman crackdown and in the dismissal of the then Party chief Zhao ziyang, who was of a younger generation in the Beijing's leadership genealogy (in fact a Deng Protégé originally) and who favored a more moderate approach to the students' movement.[2]

The tremendous influence of family relationships on Chinese society can also be indirectly seen in the role *guanx*" ("connections" or "relationships") plays in contemporary China. Although, on one level, the word *guanxi* means "network," it indicates a far stronger and closer relationship between the people involved, suggesting in essence one of an extended family. Unlike networking, which is usually confined to people in the same profession or sharing the same interest or views, *guanxi* often starts with one's relatives and family friends (especially those of your parents) and expands to include whoever may be of help to you in whatever way. So *guanxi* is far more essential in China than networking in America. When you establish a *guanxi* with a person, it implies that you have de facto included that person in your family circle, i.e. the two of you will from now on treat each other as if you were family members. You would be obligated to help each other the best you can. In China, an individual's success in a career, be it in politics, business, or other professions, depends, to a great extent, on the *guanxi* that person has cultivated. This may help explain the rampant gossip in China in the last decade about the "Shanghai Gang" having taken over the leadership in China (both Jiang Zemin, the President, and Zhu Rongji, the Premier, worked as the heads of the Shanghai city government before they took charge in the central government), and about how the Shanghai Gang has successfully purged the Beijing Gang and the Guangdong gang from the central government. The gossip is not without some grounds since Jiang and Zhu have successfully replaced the entire city government leadership of Beijing and put the former mayor and the Party chief in prison on corruption charges.

For a state-family to function properly, it requires not only an authoritative power on the part of the patriarch—the ruler—but also submission or loyalty to the ruler on the part of the citizens. Traditional

Chinese culture ensures both. As the cornerstone of Chinese culture, "Confucianism treated the family as the key unit in human society, and filial piety—loyalty and reverence towards one's parents—as the most important part of family relationships. A man's loyalty to his parents was supposed to take precedence over everything else. . ." (Moise, 1994, p.12). Such filial loyalty and reverence promoted in Chinese culture has certainly been exemplarily manifested in Confucius' descendents—in their exceptionally good care of the grave of the family guru and in their enviable maintenance of the family genealogical records. Latourette's (1964) words regarding what Confucius' descendents have accomplished in this regard surely express the amazement and admiration of many outside China: "Where else in the world is there a grave like that of Confucius, dating back into the middle of the first millennium before Christ and through the centuries cared for by one claiming lineal descent from the far-off ancestor? Probably in no other country did so large a proportion of the population take pride in maintaining its genealogical records and profess to trace them from so remote an antiquity" (p. 573). The core of the family-centered Chinese culture is thus filial piety. From filial piety develops loyalty to *guojia* or state-family. This is because, since the state is considered one's extended family, loyalty to one's local and national governments is tantamount to loyalty to one's family and ancestors.

From this piety and loyalty develops the belief that the individual or the small individual family must always place the interest of the state-family first and be willing to make sacrifices in the interest of the big family. This belief is coupled with the ideal that as the patriarchs, the state-family rulers will take good care of their citizen-children. That is perhaps partially why, despite some resistance, the Chinese government has in general successfully implemented the "one child per family policy" and has moved forward with its economic reform aimed at improving its productivity and work efficiency, in spite of the fact that the reform has resulted in millions of workers being unemployed. Viewing themselves as the caretakers of the state-family who are working for its best interest, the current Chinese government leaders have effectively stifled any criticism from its citizen-children. In doing so, they have exerted great effort to restore and reinforce the Confucian doctrine of the patriarchic rule in society that was overlooked in the early years of the Communist state. Edward Friedman's (1995) *National Identity and Democratic Prospects in Socialist China* renders an excellent discussion on how the Communist government in the post-

Mao reform era has orchestrated a pro-Confucius campaign to legitimize its rule by preaching the patriarchal values and practice and by reaffirming the state-family cultural tradition on which China has been founded.

An editorial in the Chinese government's mouthpiece, *People's Daily* ("Yu zhi qiguo, bi xiang zhi jia [To rule the country, it is necessary to rule the family first]," 1998) clearly expresses its view that governing a country is similar to governing a family, a view that, as I quoted earlier, Mo Zi put forth about two thousand and five hundred years ago: "Ruling countries everywhere in the world is the same as ruling a family." The editorial, which was addressed to high-ranking government officials, states, "To rule and manage our country well, we must first rule and manage our family well. If we cannot even rule and manage our family well, how can we do it with our country?" The thesis of the editorial is if these government officials can take full control of their families, they then will have the moral authority in governing their citizens. Such reasoning makes good sense in China where government officials are not elected and their power as citizens' parents derives, to a great extent, from being model parents. The state-family governing style has been so strong and been in existence for so long in China that derogatory set-phrases or family metaphors have been created to describe the extreme versions of the state-family. *Jiazhangzhi* and *jiatianxia* are two of them. The phrase *Jiazhangzhi*, meaning literally "family-head ruling," is used to refer to and criticize the dictatorial style of governing. Similarly, *jiatianxia*, meaning literally ""family land under heaven," is employed to describe and condemn the practice of an extreme nepotism where a person and his family and relatives control the whole governing body. Yet in a culture where state-family ruling is taken for granted, its extreme practices, despite criticism, are still alive. Reared in such a culture, Chinese rulers, whoever they may be, will find it hard to get rid of *jiazhangzhi* even if they want to, for, ironic or hypocritical as it may sound, Chinese communist leaders including Mao Zedong have, not infrequently, called for an end to "family-head-ruling."

In this family-centered culture, the government is not the only institution molded and seen in family terms. For example, when one is in charge of a company, a store, or school, the person is said to be *dangjia* (meaning literally "managing [the] family") in that organization. When employees have control or say in their work place or when citizen do the same in a city, a county, a province, or a country, they are believed to *dangjia zhuozhu* ("managing [the] family and becoming [its] master") in the respective institutions or levels of government. To conduct governing well in any place is to *danghao jia* ("managing family well"). Any capable leader of an institution is thus often called a *hao dangjia* ("a good family manager"). Even a key player in an organization or business can also be referred to as *dangjia*. For example, after Connie Chung of ABC's *Prime Time* program received very good reviews and high ratings for her interview with Jessie Jackson's mistress (about her affair with the Afro-American civil rights activist) and her interview with Gary Condit (concerning his affair with Chandra Levy and his possible involvement with her disappearance), Wang Yun, a *China Times* writer, uses the family metaphor, *dangjia huadan* in her article to refer to Connie Chung's possible re-emergence as a top anchor. Wang Yun (2001) writes, "Because of these interviews, Connie Chung has become the winner among the news anchors this summer. Her good performance this summer may enable her to once again become *dangjia huadan* (literal meaning: "female character/role that manages [the] family" as the latter term *huadan* came from the Beijing opera used to refer to a main female character").

Similarly, a company's or any organization's assets are commonly referred to as its *jiacan* or *jiadang* ("family assets"). Furthermore, a company or institution's overall resources and assets are sometimes called its *jiadi* ("family resources"). By the same token, a person who takes over a company or any institution and then ruins it by destroying its tradition or making it bankrupt is called a *baijiazi* ("family-ruining or family-asset-draining son"). Of course, any wastrel or prodigal person is also a *baijiazi*. If a person or company goes bankrupt or broke, to use common English language, the person or company is said in Chinese colloquialism to have *qingjia danchan* ("the whole family assets are depleted"). A person's best skills are referred to as *kanjia benling* ("skills for guarding a family"). To do one's best or, to use an English metaphor, *to give it one's best shot*, is in Chinese speech to *nachu zhijide kanji benling* (put into use one's family-guarding skills). If an individual shows great familiarity with an issue or subject matter, the person is said to be *rushu jiazhen* ("enumerating one's family valuables"). Anything routine or of common occurrence or anything that someone is skillful at and can do easily is called *jiachang bianfan* ("routine and common family meal"). In the same mindset, small talk in Chinese is termed *Jiachang hua* ("common family talk"). To manage an institution's finances well by saving whatever cost possible is often referred to as *qinjian cijia* ("frugally sustain a family"). Conducting the finances of an institution is thus viewed the same as running the finances of a family.

In short, the concept of family in Chinese culture is in various ways conflated with that of state and many other institutions. As a result, Chinese speakers enjoy viewing the world and their life via the family structural frame. Many non-family issues have been coded as family matters in the Chinese language, a point I will support in the next chapter.

The importance of eating in Chinese culture

To appreciate the importance of eating to the Chinese, it is necessary to understand 1) the philosophies that have shaped Chinese culture and 2) the historical socioeconomic conditions of China. As Latourette (1964) pointed out long ago, "Of the indigenous philosophies accorded a prolonged place of honor in Chinese life, only Taoism belittled the striving for bodily comfort and sought to make men independent of the trammels of the flesh" (p. 283). Yet compared with the philosophies of Confucianism and Legalism among others, Taoism has always been a minor school of thought. The major Chinese philosophies all attach great importance to the physical aspect of life. To cite Latoutette (1964) again,

> Food, clothing, and shelter have loomed large in the objectives of the Chinese. This is necessarily true in any society. Rather more than most peoples, however, the Chinese have been this-worldly in their ideals. . . . Certainly interest in the physical basis of life has been prominent in the philosophies on which the state has acted. . . . Most of the great schools of thought of Chou [dynasty] endeavored to promote man's bodily welfare as an essential condition of all gains in morals and arts. Legalists, on whose theories Ch'in Shih Huang Ti unified the Empire, stressed the economic organization of society. Confucianism recognized the fact that if there was to be civilization the masses must not be allowed to be unclad and hungry" (p. 483).

More than two millenniums have passed since the time in which the above-mentioned philosophers lived, yet their philosophies have lived on to shape the views of even present-day Chinese rulers. For example,

Deng Xiaoping (1983, Vol. 2, p. 406) claimed, "No matter what happens in the world, everything will be okay as long as people have enough food to eat." Moreover, whenever its human rights record is criticized, the Chinese government would counter the criticism by arguing that having enough to eat is the most important human right and that China has been performing well in that regard.

Beijing also uses the same argument for not adopting democracy in China. For example, in an interview with a *New York Times* delegation, Chinese President Jiang Zemin, in answering if the Communist Party would allow other parties to compete in China, said, "[S]hould China apply the parliamentary democracy of the Western world, the only result will be that 1.2 billion Chinese people will not have enough food to eat. The result will be great chaos and should that happen it will not be conducive to world peace and stability" ("In Jiang's words,"2001, p. A8). To Jiang, for the Chinese to have enough to eat is the number one concern, more important than everything else. In fact, of all the governments whose human rights records have been castigated, Beijing, not the Kremlin (of the former Soviet Union), not even any of the poorest African nations, was the first one to use this argument in its defense and has been the most frequent and the most noted high-profile user. This fact is especially intriguing because China has in the past two decades enjoyed a much higher living standard and is economically much more viable than the rest of the countries in the group. Hence an excuse as it is, Beijing's argument that the right to have food and clothing is the most important human right must be motivated more by the cultural philosophies than by its economic and living conditions. Another example showing the unusual importance of eating/food in the Chinese philosophical view of the universe is evidenced by their traditional practice of offering food in their worship services to God (Buddha, etc.) or their dead ancestors. It is very common that Chinese leave food on an altar or a relative's grave. Obviously, in the Chinese minds, even spirits need to eat.

Of course, philosophical thinking alone cannot account for the Chinese infatuation with eating. Such an obsession has developed, to a large degree, from their unnerving knowledge and/or the experience of the food shortages that have historically plagued China. Chinese history is well known for the numerous peasants' uprisings that were caused by famines. To a people who are constantly worried about not having any or not having enough food, eating surely looms large in their consciousness. Bloomfield (1983) is right on target when she writes,

"[The Chinese] are positively obsessed with food in a way which speaks eloquently of the long years of famine and deprivation that have scarred China's history" (179). Yet historically there has been something more in the Chinese socioeconomic conditions that have made eating so prominent in Chinese culture. While the majority of the Chinese people have historically suffered from starvation, the rich have always enjoyed eating to its fullest extent and made food more than something to eat, as is tersely but vividly shown in the famous lines of a poem by Du Fu, a great poet in the Tang Dynasty: "*Zhumei jiurou chou; lu you dongshi gu*" meaning "while the aristocrats' mansions are filled with the stink of meat and wine, the streets are littered with the bones of those starved and frozen to death." Enjoying luxurious food has been a status symbol in China perhaps more than in any other place on earth. That is why a person who is popular and has influential power is often called one who *chidekai* (meaning literally "eats openly"), *chixiang* ("eat fragrance"), or *chixiande helade* ("eat fragrance and drink hot stuff").

This Chinese obsession with eating may explain an otherwise difficult-to-fathom corruption problem in China—various levels' government officials' extravagant dining in restaurants using the government's or, as referred to in America, tax-payers' money. Corruption is not unique to China, but corruption in this dining form is rather exceptional and of Chinese flavor. Each year, billions of Chinese dollars of tax-payers' money were reported to have been spent on restaurant dining. What is even more unbelievable is that, based on national and provincial government media reports, many local government (city or town) officials eat in the restaurants located within the area they govern on a "credit-basis" with no means and/or no intention to pay. Many restaurants have thus reportedly gone bankrupt because of unpaid bills from government officials. As reported in an article in the January 18 *Yangcheng Wanbo* [*Yangcheng Evening Daily*], a small town's government had a debt of 1.5 million yuan (Chinese dollars), an equivalent of about $200,000 with the current exchange rate of eight yuan for one dollar. The amount was roughly its annual budget, and the bulk of it was owed to restaurants. The article also reports that one small town restaurant claimed that its town government owed them 380,000 yuan in unpaid bills ("Shengwei shuji," 2001). In an even more shocking case, a deputy Director of Human Resources in a district of Tianjin City spent 537,000 yuan in restaurant dining during his fourteen month tenure on the job ("Yao hensha gongkuang chiye feng," 1998).

Besides, Chinese people's strong passion for eating can also be seen in the way business meals or banquets are prepared and offered. In the West, a business lunch or even a formal banquet in honoring a government or business guest is generally composed of three courses: a salad/soup, a hot entree, and desserts In sharp contrast, a Chinese banquet usually consists of eight to twelve courses, most of which are hot entrees. As a result, while Western business and government leaders and tourists visiting China often feel in awe when they see the variety and amount of food served, Chinese government and business delegations to the West are frequently dismayed at the simplicity of the banquet their hosts offer. Without understanding the cultural differences in the matter, some of the Chinese feel slighted by their hosts and complain about their hosts' stinginess, yet at the same time many of the Western guests to China are overjoyed about the "special treatment and honor" in the food served to them. The Chinese meticulousness about food may partially explain why fast food did not originate in China but in the West, especially in America. The difference between China and the West in what and how food should be served at a business dinner is a cultural and philosophical one more than anything else. In terms of resources and wealth, Americans surely can afford luxurious business meals, perhaps even more than the Chinese can.

This Chinese obsession with food has turned cooking and dining into an artistic feat to enjoy and polish. An important portion of the time during a meal, especially one for social or business functions, is devoted to evaluating and commenting on each of the dishes in terms of its *taste, smell,* and *color,* criteria for judging cooking. As Bloomfield (1983) points out, "food is perhaps the most important thing in the world to a Chinese" (168), and more importantly, "food is the poetry and passion of the Chinese . . ." (173). Here I am not suggesting that food is not very important in other cultures, nor am I implying that other peoples do not eat to enjoy but merely eat to live. What I am contending is that the epicurean purpose of eating in China is far more important than it is in many other cultures, for in many instances such purpose in China outweighs the physiological (to help sustain our life) and social functions as well. The sharp contrast between the typical Western business meal/banquet and that of the Chinese as mentioned above clearly supports my point. In the West, the main purpose of a business meal/banquet is to provide a setting for the business discussion to take place. In China, dining or enjoying eating at a business or social function is as important, if not more important, than the business discussion itself. That is perhaps why alcohol drinking is almost an indispensable part of business dining. It is considered the host's responsibility in Chinese culture to make sure that the guests not only enjoy the dishes but also drink to their capacity. They often tell their guests to both *chihao* (meaning eat well) and *hede gaoxing* or *hede kuaile* (the literal translation of which is to drink until one feels good, i.e. to enter an excited mental state that borders on being drunk). It is a Chinese belief that when in a high spirit over a great meal, a businessman is much more likely to be in a good mood to reach business deals. It is no wonder that many business deals in China are reached on the dining table, often over a glass of wine. This practice constitutes a sharp contrast to a popular one in America where, as reported in the previously cited (Chapter 4) article "Women executives find it pays to speak sports" (1997), business deals are often struck on a golf course.

The unusual importance of eating in Chinese culture can be seen in many Chinese customs and rituals. For example, as I pointed out earlier, the most common casual greeting the Chinese give to their friends and colleagues is asking whether the other person has eaten or not. More importantly, holding a large banquet that involves many relatives and guests is an important Chinese ritual in the celebration of almost every important life event from birth to death, such as birthdays, weddings, and even funerals. Of course, what food should be included in the menu is often rigid and varies from event to event. A banquet for a wedding, considered a "red happiness" event, will serve many meat dishes and wine whereas a banquet for a funeral, a "white happiness event," often offers only a vegetarian menu. As I mentioned earlier, it is also a Chinese custom to bring and leave food items on the grave when they visit their dead relatives. Those who have watched the famous Chinese movie *"To Live"* directed by Zhang Yimou will perhaps never forget the denouement where, leaving some dumplings on his son's grave, the protagonist tells the dead son to enjoy the meal. Offering food is also a common practice in more routine events. For example, traditionally, when people visit their relatives or friends, food items are the most common presents they give to their host. The same is even true when they visit people in the hospital. They usually bring the patient fruits, canned drinks, etc. rather than flowers as people in the West do. Of course, the custom is changing due to Western influences.

An equally interesting example of the unusual Chinese interest in eating is their strong belief in the medical and health functions of food. Many Chinese believe that eating animals' organs is good for human organs. For instance, a pig's heart is very good for someone who has a heart disease. The same is true of pig's kidney for kidney patients. Similarly, dried male dog's genitals are considered good for male individuals who have sexual malfunctions, and they are often used in Chinese traditional herbal medicine. Of course, the way to cook these animal organs is very particular. The organs should be whole and often should be steamed in a covered container. For the best result for heart patients, people often place a gold ring in the animal's heart when steaming it. Many Chinese also believe in a relationship between the food that one eats, including the way it is cooked and the kind of life and luck one may have. Of course, the actual specific beliefs and customs vary from region to region. For example, in many parts of China, the Chinese New Year's Eve dinner, the most important meal of the year, should include a whole fish, but it should not be touched or at least not finished because the pronunciation of the Chinese word fish, "*yu,*" is the same as that of the Chinese word "surplus." They want their family to have surplus carrying over to the next year. Similarly, celery should also be on the menu of this important dinner because the Chinese word celery is a homophone with the word for industry "*qin.*" They eat it in the belief that they will be industrious the following year. They also include on the menu *yuto*, a small round potato-like produce, because its shape resembles that of Chinese gold nuggets. They want to be prosperous in the coming year, too.

These kinds of practices concerning food eating, especially the eating of animal organs, often form both a cultural model parallel to and a source for some linguistic eating metaphors. For example, a common Chinese expression to suggest that a person is unusually or brazen bold is that the person *chi le baozi dan* ("has eaten a panther's gallbladder"). It is a firm Chinese belief that panthers, like tigers and lions, are brave and bold and that boldness and braveness all come from one's gallbladder. Based on the Chinese belief mentioned above that the eating of an animal organ is beneficial to the counterpart human organ, it follows that eating a panther's gallbladder should give one enormous boldness. It is in the same mentality that, because of tiger's known might, Chinese for thousands of years have used tiger bones to help make wines for nourishing human bones and strength.

Chinese are also extremely particular about keeping a balance in diet, not the balance in the typical Western sense, though, but a balance between *ying* and *yang*. According to Chinese traditional philosophy, the world exists in peace and order via keeping a balance between the forces of *ying* and *yang*. Similarly based on Chinese traditional medicine, human beings keep fit by maintaining in the body a balance of *ying* and *yang*. One way to help us maintain such a balance is to eat a diet of equal amounts of *ying* and *yang*. Food items in China are divided into *ying* and *yang* with turtle, duck, yam etc. falling into the former category and beef, lamb, and pepper, among others, being classified as the latter. This strong belief about a balanced diet for good health has been extended to life in general, figuratively of course. For example, *pian shi* ("unbalanced diet") has been a popular metaphor to refer to one-sidedness in any matter.

All the above discussion about the Chinese people's obsession with food has clearly showed that eating occupies an unusually important place in Chinese people's life. With eating looming so large in their consciousness, the Chinese often tend to view life as, above all, an eating event and to use eating metaphors extensively in their discourse, as shown in the metaphors mentioned at the beginning of the chapter: "*eat a defeat*," "*eat a lawsuit*," "*eat a surprise*," "*eat a loss*," "*eat fragrance* [being popular and able to throw one's weight around]." Indeed, life experience as an eating event is best evidenced by the fact that the word "eat" in all these expressions can be substituted with the word "experience" without change of meaning at all, for "eating defeats, surprises, losses, etc." is none other than "experiencing them." It is with this life-as-eating mentality that Deng Xiaoping, in discussing the horrors of the tumultuous ten-year Cultural Revolution and the need for stability and unity in China, said, "In the past, we already *ate* more than ten years of *kutou* ["bitterness", meaning hardships and sufferings]. If chaos and instability are allowed again, people *chi buxiao* ["cannot eat and digest it any more," meaning "cannot stand it any more"]" (1983, Vol. 2, p. 252). It is also in this mentality that Xia Zhen, a reporter of Taiwan's *China Times*, calls the conclusion of Taiwan's 1998 "three-in-one" election (elections at the national, provincial and county levels simultaneously) "the end of an exciting and emotional banquet" (Xia, 1998). Similarly, when asked why *Crouching Tiger, Hidden Dragon* gained such a warm reception in the West by winning four Oscars but received only a tepid response in China and the Far East, Jiang Wen, a famous Chinese actor and director, replied, "Chinese have been used to eating the same dish, but Westerners haven't, so when they take a bite of it, they find it very refreshing" (Jiang, Zhaolun, 2001). To many Chinese, life is indeed eating, a notion that Cui Yongyuan, a famous anchor at China's Central TV, vividly expresses when he makes the following comment about life, "Life is *jiaozi* [dumpling with fillings]; the years one spent in life are the wrapping, and the life experiences one has had are the fillings, which contains the entire spectrum of taste: sweet, sour, bitter, hot and all" ("Cui Yongyuan: Woduo zhongguo," 2001).

Notes

1. Some of the following discussion on the Chinese concept of *Guojia* and its impact on Chinese culture is based on a previously published article: Liu, D. and Lin C. (1999).

2. In fact, Deng Xiaoping, in several his now published speeches, explicitly admitted the critical role he and his octogenarian colleagues played (1993, Vo. 3, pp. 302-303, 324). Of course, the Communist regime is not the first Chinese government where members of an old generation without legitimate official titles exercise a decisive power. For example, the Dowager Empress Cixi (1835-1908) acted as the de facto ruler of China by governing behind the doors during her son Tongzhi's reign (1862-1874) and her nephew Guangxu's reign (1875-1908).

Chapter 7

"Relatives or Neighbors" and *"Married-Out Daughters"*: Relationships between Mainland China and Taiwan, and Ties between China and the Overseas Chinese

> "Taiwan and [mainland] China are distant relatives but close neighbors."
> --Lü Hsiu-lien, Vice President of ROC in Taiwan
>
> "The overseas Chinese are married-out daughters of China."
> --Zhou Enlai, Late Premier of China

As already explained in the previous chapter, family metaphors figure prominently in the Chinese language, especially in its political and business discourse. In this chapter, I will try to support my claim by exploring how family metaphors have been used in defining and framing the Taiwan issue--the relationship between Mainland China and Taiwan--and in describing and shaping China's relationship with the overseas Chinese, two very important issues to the Chinese government and its people in their drive for unifying and modernizing their country. Let us first look at the debate or quarrel between Beijing and Taiwan over the status of Taiwan. For us to better understand the issue, a little historical background is in order.

China ceded Taiwan to Japan in 1895 after its defeat in the first Sino-Japanese war. At the end of World War II, Japan returned Taiwan to China, then ruled by the Nationalist Government. When the

Communists took over Mainland China in 1949, the Nationalist government retreated to Taiwan. Since then, the Communist government and the Nationalist government have been ruling Mainland China and Taiwan respectively and separately with each forming a de facto political entity. The Beijing government has all along claimed to be the sole legitimate government of China, including Taiwan. Until the early 1990s, the Nationalist government held the same position. The two sides conducted a formal talk in 1992 to discuss the relationship between them with each side adhering to a one-China policy although differing on what constitutes this one China and what each government is entitled to with regard to the entire China. In other words, both sides agreed that both the Mainland and Taiwan belong to China. Yet since the independence-minded Lee Teng-hui took over the reign of the government in Taiwan and consolidated his power, he began to move away from the one-China policy that his predecessors held, although he and his government never openly declared independence. A heated quarrel has ensued between Beijing and Taiwan over the definition of the relationship between the two sides. The quarrel has, on several occasions, almost amounted to war. For instance, Beijing launched large war games involving the shooting of missles over Taiwan in 1995 in an angry response to Lee Teng-hui's visit to the United States. Fortunately because of some restraints on both sides and the intervention of other countries, the fight between the two sides has remained in words. This rhetorical play is the interest of my study here.

In this war of words, each side wants to convince the other and its people that its position is the right one, and they have resorted to the arguments and rhetoric that they believe best appeal to the general public on both sides of the Taiwan Straight. Despite their independence position, the Taiwanese side, or, to be more accurate, those for independence in Taiwan (since not all residents of Taiwan favor independence), cannot deny that they share the same language[1] and basically the same culture with the Chinese in the Mainland. It is for this reason, I argue, that the two sides, in spite of their opposing positions, converge on the use of family metaphors in their debate. As stated earlier, Beijing has, from the beginning, held the position that Taiwan is part of China and the Beijing government is the only legitimate government of the entire China. Its rhetoric has thus remained consistent and has been anchored on Taiwan being part of the Chinese family. For example, they have been consistently addressing the Taiwanese people as *tongbao*, meaning literally "persons born of the same parents." Often, to emphasize an extremely close relationship between the two sides, the term *tongbao* has been used with an adjectival *gurou* ("bones and flesh"), hence *gurou tongbao*, meaning "people of the same parents sharing bones and flesh." Both terms figured prominently in the two most important Chinese official statements regarding Taiwan, one made in 1979 by Ye Jianying, the late Chairman of the People's Congress and the other in 1995 by Jiang Zemin, the current Chinese President. The former is often known as "Ye's Nine–point Statement," and the latter is frequently referred to as "Jiang's Eight-point Statement."

For example, the seventh point of Jiang's Eight-point Statement reads, "The twenty one million Taiwanese *tongbao*, whether of Taiwanese provincial origin or other provincial origin, are all Chinese. All are our *gurou tongbao* (people of the same parents sharing bones and blood), and all are our brothers as close as one's hands and feet. [We] must respect the lifestyle of the Taiwanese *Tongbao* and respect their wish to *danjia zuozhu* ("managing [their] family and be [their own] masters," i.e. "be in control of their own fate and affairs"), and to safeguard all the normal rights of the Taiwanese *tongbao*" (Jiang, 1995, p. 258). In this passage, Jiang makes use of not only the *tongbao* and *gurou tongbao* family metaphors but also the family metaphor, *dangjia zuozhu* ("manage [the] family and be [one's own] master") when he says that the Chinese government respects the Taiwanese people's "wish to *dangjia zuozhu*." The effort to appeal to the people of a family-centered culture is very obvious. Yet the irony is that this latter family metaphor appears to undermine the validity of the first one linguistically. If the Taiwanese belong to the family of China, how can they truly manage their own family affairs? Conversely, if they have their own family to manage, then there will be two separate families: the China family and the Taiwan family. Obviously, Beijing is either not aware of the ironic linguistic contradiction or does not care since in Beijing's mentality, Taiwan is part of the Chinese family and that is what matters. Beijing even argues that the "one-China but two system" policy (Socialism in the Mainland but capitalism in Taiwan) that it has advocated since the 1980s is designed, in its Vice Premier and foreign affairs chief Qian Qichen's words, "to respect and satisfy the Taiwanese people's strong desire to *dangjia zuozhu*," ("Zai jilian Jiang Zemin duitai zhongyao jianghua liu zhounian huishangdi jianghua [Speech at the gathering marking the sixth anniversary of Jiang Zemin's important statement about Taiwan]," 2001).

Beijing's use of family metaphors to define and shape the Taiwan issue is not confined to its communication with Taiwan. It figures prominently in its exchanges with the rest of the world. For example, in addressing the U.S.-Sino Relations National Committee at a lunch in his honor while attending the UN General Assembly, Chinese President Jiang Zemin made the following comments regarding the Taiwan issue: "Taiwan has been part of China since ancient times. To achieve the unification of the motherland [Mainland China and Taiwan] is the common will of all the *zhonghua ernu* (a family metaphor meaning "the Chinese sons and daughters) both home and abroad. Chinese people love peace and most hate to see wars between *tongbao* brothers. . ." (*"Taiwan shi zhong mei guanxi zui zhongyao de wenti* [Taiwan is the most important issue in Sina-America relationship]," 2000)

Beijing's use of the family metaphor has sometimes taken on a personal flavor. In an open letter (dated July 24, 1982) addressed to Chiang Ching-Kuo, the late President of the Republic of China in Taiwan (1976 to 1988), Liao Chenzhi, the late Vice Chair of the Chinese People's Congress, quoted a couplet from a famous poem by Lu Xun, one of the most famous Chinese writers in the twentieth century, to suggest and emphasize brotherhood between the two of them personally and between the two sides at large. The couplet reads, *jiebo yujin xiongdi zai, xiangfeng yixiao mian ancho*, meaning "after waves of calamities [indirectly referring to the wars between the Communists and the Nationalists], we brothers are still alive. Let's meet and smile to dissolve our grudges." Such explicit appeal to brotherhood certainly helps make the argument for unification stronger. *Tongbao, gurou tongbai*, and *xiongdi* ("brothers") are not the only family metaphors that Beijing has used to define the relation between Mainland China and Taiwan. In less formal talks and meetings, Chinese officials have employed less formal terms such as *zijiaren, yijiaren, or jialiren*, all meaning "members within the family." For example, in an interview with Taiwan's *Zhongshi* (*China TV*), Lee Kuan Yew, former Prime Minister and current Senior Minister of Singapore, a friend of both Beijing and Taiwan and a believed go-between for the two sides, said that "Since 1996, Mainland China has stated its stance that the problem between the two sides across the [Taiwan] Strait is a *family issue* and that I'm not their *zijiaren* [member within the family] so I should not intervene" ("Lee Kuan Yew: liangan," 2000). Lee repeated the message that Beijing told him in an interview with America's United Press International ("Lee Kuan Yew jieshou zhuanfang," 2001).

Chinese officials often stated the same thing using the same language when they visited the U.S. Mingxi Wu, the head of a Chinese delegation attending a conference on Beijing-Taiwan relations in Los Angeles, was quoted, in Chen Hongyi's report in *Zhongguo Ribao*'s [*China Daily*, a Chinese newspaper in America], to say that "The Taiwan issue is a matter within the Chinese *family* and outsiders should not be allowed to interference" (Chen Hongyi, 2000). Similarly, Chinese officials have reiterated numerous times that, following the Chinese principle and tradition of not fighting and killing *zhijiaren* ("members of the same family"), Beijing's threat of using forces against Taiwan is not targeted at the Taiwanese people but at foreign forces that intend to control Taiwan. It is clear that Beijing has sought every opportunity to remind the world that people in both mainland China and Taiwan are all descendants of the same ancestor, hence members of the same family.

Following this line of thinking, Beijing's media have repeatedly accused Taiwan's independence-seeking politicians of being *shudian wang zu* ["forgetting (their) ancestors in discussing history"] and branded them *baijiazi* or *minzu bailei*. Of the latter two Chinese terms, *baijiazi*, as explained in the previous chapter, means literally a "family-ruining son" and, for lack of a true equivalent in English, it has often been loosely translated as "prodigal," "spendthrift," or "wastrel." *Minzu bailei* means "scum of a nation." A very interesting point that needs to be made here is that while the Chinese leaders like to condemn the independence-minded leaders as *baijiazhi* or *minzhu bailei*, they themselves face the same condemnation if they allow Taiwan to become independent. It is one of the major reasons that all Chinese leaders, regardless of their stance on other political issues, sound hawkish on the Taiwan issue. In a family-centered culture, *baijiazhi* or *minzu bailei* is the last thing one wants to be labeled as. Based on the above discussion, it is clear that Beijing has attempted on every front to frame the across-the-Taiwan Straight relationship as that of a family. By using the family metaphors, Beijing aims to appeal to the most important Chinese traditional virtue-- piety and loyalty to one's ancestors--and in the process defines the relationship between the two sides in vivid concrete terms that resonate loudly in the Chinese consciousness or psyche. Of course, such play by Beijing has not always been well received in Taiwan, especially when Beijing tries to act as if it were the "patriarch" of Taiwan. For example, after Yu Keli, Deputy Director of Beijing's Institute of Research on Taiwan and the head of a Beijing's delegation to Taiwan, severely criticized Taiwan's Vice President while in Taiwan, Hu Zhiqiang, former Foreign Minister of Taiwan, complained that "Yu Keli feels like he was speaking in the Mainland and there were no spatial difference between the two places. He is wrong, and he shouldn't feel that *tianxia dou shi wo de jia* ["all under the heaven is my family"]" (Ma Dao-rong, 2001). To a large number of Taiwanese, Taiwan lies beyond the family of China, at least for now.

What is most intriguing concerning this war of words between Beijing and Taiwan is that Beijing is not the only one that has been resorting to the family metaphor rhetoric. So has Taiwan, even though it is in no mood or hurry to join the Beijing family, to say the least. In fact, both the pro-unification and the independence-minded politicians in Taiwan have joined in this rhetorical play and they all try to play it to Taiwan's advantage, though from different angles. While Beijing uses the family metaphor to appeal to the Taiwanese residents and support the argument that, being members of the same family, the Mainland and Taiwan are one nation and should seek unification, Taiwan, on the other hand, plays with the metaphor to, I contend, shield itself from Beijing's threat to use forces for unification and to soften Beijing's aggressive attitude towards Taiwan. The rationale is that as family members, both sides should be very friendly to each other and solve their differences by discussion, not by force. A look at Taiwan's use of family metaphors in this war of words in the past decade will illustrate the point. As pointed out earlier, until the late 1980s, the Nationalist government in Taiwan maintained that it was the only legitimate government of the entire Chinese territory, including Mainland China and Hong Kong. After Lee Teng-hui succeeded Chiang Ching-Kuo as the chief of the Nationalist Party and the President of ROC, he began a very gradual shift in the position. First, he abandoned the claim that Taipei was the only legitimate government of entire China and, instead, maintained that Beijing and Taipei were two equal political entities in the Chinese territory. Yet in 1998, two years before the end of his administration, he changed his position again by announcing informally in an interview with a German reporter that the relationship between Mainland China and Taiwan was a "special nation to nation" one. Regardless of these position changes, Lee and his officials, throughout his administration, continuously resorted to the family metaphor to simultaneously advance their course and protect themselves.

Very often, the Taiwanese leaders, including Lee, defined the relationship between the two sides as one between family members. For example, in Lee's now famous official Six-point Statement regarding the relationship in question, Lee Ten-Hui referred to the residents on both sides of the Taiwan Strait as flesh-blood relatives and called the relationship between the two sides *xiongdi guangxi* ("brother to brother") ("Liangan xiongde guanxi," 1995, p. A1). Furthermore, his fifth point starts with the following: "The children and grand children [descendants] of Yanhuan [the first emperor of China] must show sincerity and should not *gurou xiangcan* ("bones and flesh kill each other")" and the beginning of his sixth point reads, "Hong Kong and Macau are Chinese territories. The residents of Hong Kong and Macau are our bone-flesh brothers, too . . ." ("Lee Teng-hui huiying," 1995, p. A2). The theme could not be clearer: as close family members, Beijing and Taiwan should not resort to force to solve their differences.

Lee's play with the family metaphor was very skilful. While in public, especially to audiences outside Taiwan, Lee defined the relationship as one between brothers; in private or in his own circle, however, he called it a father-son relationship with Taiwan being the father and Beijing the son. Such a metaphorical maneuver was likely aimed to score points with his constituencies and also to help him gain a psychological upper hand in his dealing with Beijing. Commenting on the Beijing-Taiwan relations in a speech to a training session of his party's (The Nationalist Party) activists, Lee claimed, "We (Taiwan) are the father; the Chinese Communist government is the son. There is no such a thing for the son to take control before the father is dead" (Lee Teng-hui shuo, 1995, p. A1). Surprising as it is, Lee's claim of the Nationalist Party being the father is not without any ground, for the Republic of China, the title of the Nationalist government, was founded in 1911, long before the Communist government known as the People's Republic of China (established in 1949). Lee Teng-hui repeated the claim many times, even after he changed his stance on the relationship. In an interview with a Japanese news magazine in 1999, Lee was quoted to say, "The relationship between our two sides is a special nation-to-nation one, and The Republic of China in Taiwan is the father while the Mainland is the son" ("Lee Teng-hui zhi tai shi fuqin," 1999). This statement of Lee's does not sound logical or is far fetched at best because the father-son metaphor in essence is incompatible with the nation-to-nation position. This self-contradictory rhetoric could only be seen as Lee's strategic move to simultaneously advocate independence for Taiwan and guard against Beijing's attack because it is considered a great sin in Chinese culture not to respect your parents and ancestors. As a son, Beijing would be considered to lack filial piety if it attacked Taiwan.

Compared with Lee Teng-hui' play with family metaphors on the issue, the current Taiwanese President Chen Shui-bian and Vice President Lü Shiu-Lian's play is equally, if not more, adept and intriguing. Both Chen and Lü are members of the Democratic Progressive Party that has openly advocated independence for Taiwan. They campaigned and won as their party's candidates. Before they were elected, they stated that Taiwan was an independent country and they defined the relationship between Beijing and Taiwan metaphorically as *yuanqin jinlin* ("distant relatives but close neighbors"). This definition takes into consideration the ethnic ties and geographic proximity between the two sides but denies a close relationship: not brothers nor father-son but "distant relatives." Beijing was extremely furious at such a definition and considered it an attempt to separate Taiwan from the Mainland. They condemned it through various means such as newspaper editorials, press conferences, and officials' speeches. They even personally attached Chen and Lü, Lü in particular, as *minju bailei* ("scum of the nation."). Chen Shui-bian understood Beijing's rage in the matter.

After he won the election, especially immediately before his inauguration, Chen softened and even tried to conceal his Taiwan-independence stance by switching his metaphor for the Beijing-Taiwan relationship from that of "distant relatives" to that of "close relatives" and "family members" like "brothers and sisters." In a video conference with his "senior advisors" on May 17, 2000, three days before his inauguration, Chen stated, "The two sides across the Taiwan Straight are of the same family, are close relatives, as close as brothers and sisters. Only if the two sides cooperate can the family be harmonious. This is the foundation of any success" ("Chen Shui-bian: Haixia liangan," 2000). He was quoted in the speech to appeal to Beijing for abandoning the threat of use of force against Taiwan. On the same day, in another speech he made while visiting Hsie Tong-Min, Senior Counsel to the President, he reiterated that the two sides were members of the same family and only through cooperation would the family be harmonious and prosperous, and he further stressed that members of a family must entertain close and intimate feelings and stay close. He also stated that if the two sides resorted to force and nurture antagonism in dealing with each other, then family members would become strangers (Chen Shui-bian cheng liangan, 2000). The statements by Chen cited above indicate clearly that Chen's switch to the use of the metaphor of "close family members" was intended above all to fend off Beijing's threat of use of force against Taiwan.

Another family metaphor that Taiwanese politicians and media figures have used is related to marriage. A lead in a news report by Wang Li-juan, *Shijie Ribao*'s special reporter in Beijing, provides a very good example. The lead reads

> At the 1998 Conference on the Cross-the-Straight Relationship held in Beijing, both Shao Yu-Min, Director of International Center of the [Taiwan's] Politics University, and Yao Chia-Wen, the former Chairman of [Taiwan's] Democratic Progressive Party, coincidentally used the dating relationship to describe the relationship between the two sides. Shao Yu-Min argued that as in dating, it takes time for the two sides across the Straight to develop their relationship. Beijing should not hurriedly pressure Taiwan into marriage. Yao, on the other hand, contended that Taiwan was an entity in existence independent of China. It should be made clear that Taiwan was not Beijing's wife. As for whether [Taiwan] should form matrimony with the Mainland, it had to be decided by the people of Taiwanese." (Wang, Li-juan, 1998, p. A2).

The implied message of both speakers cited is that Taiwan is not part of China, at least not yet. While Shao and Yao used the dating metaphor, Li Ao, a famous writer and TV commentator in Taiwan, compared the two sides to that of an estranged couple. According to an interview with Li by Annie Huang of the Associated Press, "Comparing the rival governments [Beijing and Taipei] to an estranged couple, Li said China would allow Taiwan to have extramarital affairs but would never approve a formal divorce" (Huang, 2000). Even Lü Hsiu-lien, the current Vice President of Taiwan, on several occasions said Taiwan was the abused spouse and Beijing was the abuser. She accused Beijing of behaving as a male Chauvinist treating Taiwan as an unequal spouse.[2] Like Beijing's self-contradictory claim that it respects the Taiwanese people's strong desire to *dangjia zuozhu* ("manage [their] family and be [their own] master") but simultaneously wants Taiwan to be part of the China family, Lü's use of the abused wife metaphor also contradicts her claim that Taiwan is not part of China but a distant relative. Spouses are not distant relatives. They are, on the contrary, close and intimate family members. These examples of self-contradictory metaphors help to accentuate the popularity of the family metaphors in Chinese culture. Speakers like to resort to popular expressions in order to better appeal to their audience, but they often run the risk of overusing or even misusing them without knowing it.

Even the overseas Chinese, who are no longer citizens of China, view the Mainland China and Taiwan relationship in family terms. For example, in an article in *Shijie Zhoukan (a weekly* of *Shijie Ribao*) regarding the relationship between Beijing and Taiwan, Cao Zhi-yuan, a professor of political science at Southern Methodist University, writes,

> At present, the two sides across the straight differ greatly in their view on the issue [the two sides' status in their relationship], for Taiwan wants to be treated as an equal but Beijing brands itself as the Central government. In [Chinese] history, there were many stories of rulers voluntarily yielding their power to those under them: fathers yielding to their sons and older brothers yielding to their younger brother, and even men conceding to women. If Beijing has the courage and humility, she should not throw her weight around as the central government and should respect the economically successful Taiwan rather than relegating it to a secondary-partner status. Does that hurt any of Beijing's real power? No! (Cao Zhi-yuan, 1995, p. S3).

This appeal to the sense of both sides being of one family when they are engaged in ethnic or regional conflicts is a unique Chinese practice. Such appeal has seldom been used as the main argument in the fight against separation movements in other countries.

Now let us turn to China's use of family metaphors in defining and shaping her relationship with the overseas Chinese.[3] The ties of the overseas Chinese to China are arguably closer than those of any other overseas ethnic groups to the country of their origin. The numerous Chinatowns and the many Chinese *tongxiang hui* (associations of Chinese from the same province or same town) are a good testimony to their affinity to their native culture. More importantly, the overseas Chinese have exhibited an unconditional and almost blind loyalty to China, or to be more accurate, to the Beijing government--the state of China, a loyalty that does not very often exist among other overseas ethnic groups towards their native countries. In fact, the attitude of the majority of the overseas Chinese towards Beijing forms a sharp contrast with that of the immigrants from other communist countries to their governments. For example, the majority of Cuban Americans have been pushing for tougher U.S. policies to isolate the Castro regime and pressuring the U.S. government to adopt more severe measures to punish Havana. So did most immigrants from the former Soviet Union and the East European Communist countries during the Cold War era. Similarly, the Vietnamese American community at large has also stood firm against the Hanoi government. There have been many reported incidents in different cities where the Vietnamese community launched fierce, sometimes violent, attacks on stores that hung the Communist Vietnam's flag. They even would not allow the U.S. government to do things that may be construed as supporting the Hanoi government. To quote an August 12, 2001 AP report, "The [U.S.] Postal service says it will discard brochures showing the Vietnamese flag because a San Jose Vietnamese group protested the use of the communist national symbol. The multilingual pamphlet, 'A world of Services to Meet Your Needs,' used national flags to denote text in English, Italian, Tagalog, Polish, Spanish, Vietnamese and Korean" ("Vietnamese Flag dropped off brochure," 2001, p. A22).

In contrast to what Cuban and Vietnamese Americans do, Chinese Americans, except for a small minority, actively lobby for Beijing on a variety of issues including trade, Taiwan, and the bid to hold the Olympic games despite Beijing's poor human rights record and other problems. For instance, concerning the hotly debated issue in the 1990s of whether the U.S. should grant China the Most Favored Nation trade status (MFN), the Chinese American community overwhelmingly supported it, and, as Ellingwood, (1997) pointed out, the support cut across many different political and ideological camps, including many exiled dissidents. What is more shocking to many Americans is that the Chinese American community often will not allow any criticism of Beijing. For example, the overseas Chinese launched vehement protests when NBC's Bob Costas criticized China's human rights problems in his introduction of the Chinese delegation at the Atlanta Olympics in 1996. The network later had to apologize, in its spokesman's words, to the Chinese Americans not "for facts in Bob's remarks, but rather for the feelings that were hurt" ("Nothing to be sorry for," 1996)—the feelings, I would argue, of pride and loyalty that the overseas Chinese hold for China.

An interesting question to ask here is what has led to this strong overseas Chinese loyalty to China. One reason, I would like to argue, is the influence of the conflation of family and state and the view of filial piety as the highest virtue, unique features of Chinese culture that I have already described and explained. Chinese are expected to be loyal not only to their ancestors but also to the state since the state is the extended family of individual families. This loyalty to the state, as Elegant (1959, p. 14) pointed out years ago, has always been

> as binding as the coils of mortality: death alone can dissolve the individual's compact with nature and death alone can release the Chinese from his obligation to the motherland . . . . Despite Revolutions, Republics, Communism and Capitalism, the bond today remains as it was in the past. Profound economic or political crisis may drive a Chinese into voluntary exile, the state of the overseas Chinese. But as long as he thinks of himself as Chinese, no power can release the sojourner from service to China.

Furthermore, any individual who has done anything that may be perceived harmful to the state is often considered a disloyal person, a traitor, and would be condemned accordingly. A good example is the response of many overseas Chinese to Harry Wu, who has tried to expose labor camps and other human rights violations in China, and Zhang Yimou, a famous Chinese film director who was already mentioned in the previous chapter and whose films have largely explored the negative sides of Chinese culture and humanity at large. To these overseas Chinese, Wu and Zhang have brought shame to China, whether or not their stories were true and regardless of the aesthetic value of Zhang's work, because both have violated a Chinese taboo: *jiachou buko waiyang* ("Domestic scandals should not be exposed to outsiders"). In fact, it has become a common scene in America that when Chinese dissidents gather to protest against visiting Chinese leaders or Chinese policies, many overseas Chinese would yell at them, calling them "traitors."

Historically, the Chinese governments, starting from the Qing dynasty to the current Beijing region, have played extensively with the family metaphor to heighten the overseas Chinese sense of being part of the China family while away from China. As we recall, Chinese rulers like to call all ethnic Chinese, home and abroad, *zhonghua ernu* ("sons and daughters of China") or *yanhuang zisun* ("the children and grandchildren of yan [the first Chinese] Emperor"). For example, it has almost become a bible-quoting-like practice for Beijing officials to say that "*zhonghua ernu* all over the world are against any attempt to make

Taiwan independent" or "*yanhuang zisun* will never allow Taiwan to be taken away from China." In order to help overseas Chinese always remember their origin and remain loyal to China, the Qing Imperial Government coined the term *hua-qiao* (*hua* is the short word form for China and *qiao* means sojourner, hence "China sojourner") to refer to all overseas Chinese, replacing the various terms that overseas Chinese had been using to call themselves such as *min yue ren* (people from Guandong and Fujian provinces (G. Wang, 1991). This new term with the character *hua* affirmed a direct link between these people and China, and signified that "the *huaqiao* owed their allegiance to China and the Qing State (and after 1911, to the Republic) and [it] entailed certain legal rights and responsibilities towards the Chinese state" (Ong and Nonini, 1997, p. 42).

Since coming to power in 1949, the Communist government has adopted a new metaphor to refer to the overseas Chinese: *zhongguo jiacuqude nuer* ("the married-out daughters of China"). It is an interesting and thoughtful metaphor on the part of Beijing. It not only emphasizes the ethnic origin of the overseas Chinese and their responsibilities, but it also recognizes the fact that these people are no longer citizens or residents of China. According to Chinese custom, married-out daughters should maintain affinity with their parents by regularly *huei niangjia* (visiting their parents). It has been a well-established and faithfully followed tradition. Hence like married-out daughter, the overseas Chinese are supposed to keep close ties to China. The "married-out daughters" metaphor has figured prominently in Beijing's discourse with the overseas Chinese. It has been the buzzword in many of the meetings between Chinese officials and the leaders of the overseas Chinese communities in America and other countries. By referring to themselves as China's "married-out daughters," the overseas Chinese have, consciously and unconsciously, assumed the duties and responsibilities that the term implies they have towards China. In fact, Beijing's choice of the "married-out daughters" metaphor for the overseas Chinese has another undertone. According to Chinese tradition, married-out daughters have to show loyalty to their parents but they no longer have a say in their parents' family business. In that sense, they are second-class family members. By the same token, the overseas Chinese are also secondary members of the China family, for they are expected to show loyalty to China but are not supposed to become too involved with her family business. This latter stipulation may in part help explain why Beijing has been reportedly keeping a close eye on the overseas Chinese who return to China for a visit or other business.

In summary, family metaphors figure prominently in the Chinese political discourse. They also appear frequently in Chinese people's daily conversation such as *"Zeer shui dangjia?"* ("who is managing [the] family here?") to mean who is in charge and *"jiachang bianfan"* ("routine family meal") to mean something common. As I pointed out at the beginning in Chapter 6, even though the number of family metaphors in Chinese is not enormous especially in comparison with that of eating metaphors, they are extremely important as they reveal how the Chinese view some of the fundamental aspects of life and society.

Notes

1. Linguists do not quite agree whether the Southern Min [Fujian Province] language spoken by most residents of Taiwan is a dialect of Chinese or a separate language. The fact is that, like many other Chinese dialects or languages, the written form of the Southern Min language is Chinese although its speech (especially pronunciation) differs significantly from Mandarin, the officially-declared standard Chinese language.

2. For Lü's comments on this issue in detail, see an interview with her by Li Ge, special reporter of the U.S. office of Hong Kong's *Singtao Ribao* (Li, 2000), and a news report by Chen Ying-ying of Taiwan's Central News Agency about Lü's speech at a conference held in Taiwan's Central Research Academy (Chen, Ying-ying., 2000).

3. The following discussion on the relationships between China and the overseas Chinese has drawn extensively from a previously published article: Liu, D. and Lin, C. (1999).

Chapter 8

Human-Eating Society and *Case-Eating Police*: The use of eating metaphors in Chinese

> "*Dagaimao* [the type of uniform caps that Chinese judicial officers such as judges, prosecutors, and police wear--a synecdoche referring to police and judges] *eat their plaintiffs first and then eat the defendants.*"
> --A line from a very famous Chinese doggerel satirizing judicial corruptions in China
>
> "*Chi an* [eating cases] is an important part of the police job."
> --A claim by many police officers in Taiwan

As pointed out in Chapter 6, eating has historically occupied a central place in the life of the Chinese, much more so than it has in the lives of the people of many other cultures. Due to the unusual importance of food and eating in Chinese culture, eating constitutes a dominant metaphor in the Chinese language. To further support my point, I will explore how the eating metaphor has been extensively used in depicting human behavior and social evils in China and in portraying governing practices. An in-depth analysis of the use of the eating metaphor in this area will, I believe, help to illustrate Chinese people's tendency to view the world and human behavior in terms of eating and to reveal a proximity in the Chinese consciousness between eating and practices that, in the mind of people of other languages, have little do with eating.

There are many eating metaphors in the Chinese language that deal with human behavior. Here are just a few examples: *chi cu* ("to eat vinegar") meaning to be jealous; *chili pawai* ("to eat inside but scoop things outside") meaning "to live off one person while secretly helping another"; *Chruan bu chiyin* ("to eat softness but not hardness") meaning to accept or be open to gentle persuasion but not coercion; *chibulia douzhe zou* ("to not be able to finish all the requested food and therefore have to take the food home by carrying it in the lap") meaning to ask for trouble or to get oneself in trouble, similar to the English idiom "to get more than one bargained for"; *yin chou* ("to drink hatred") meaning to nurture/harbor hatred. Because of limited space, I will confine my discussion in this chapter to a few eating metaphors that depict social evils, immoral behaviors, and governing. In the Introduction (Chapter 1), I already mentioned one such metaphor--*chi renxue mantou* ("eat steamed bread soaked with blood"), which is used to describe the behavior of gaining or benefiting from the tragedy of other peoples' deaths. Vivid and shocking as it is, this metaphor is not very often used because the situations that warrant its use are not very common. A far better-known and far more widely used one is *chiren de shehui* ("human-eating society"), a metaphorical term referring to an unjust society that ruthlessly destroys human beings both spiritually and physically. I will first focus my exploration on this metaphor and a few others along with it because it has been extensively used in many Chinese literary works to help expose the evils in the Chinese society. I will then explore another eating metaphor, *chi an* ("eating cases"), one that has been widely used to refer to the police practice of suppressing or under-reporting criminal cases to make their job performance look better. Finally, I conclude the chapter by examining the use of eating metaphor to portray governing practices.

Let us first look at the use of *chiren de shihui* ("man-eating society"). The story entitled "A Madman's Diary" by Lu Xun, one of the most renowned Chinese writers in the twentieth century, provides an excellent example. In this story, Lu Xun aims to unmask the evils of the feudal society through an insane man's unique vision and understanding of his family and the society at large. The following are excerpts from the story translated by X. Yang and G. Yang (1981).

"A Madman's Diary"

. . . .

III

. . . .

The most extraordinary thing was that woman on the street yesterday who was spanking her son. "Little devil!" she cried. "I'm so angry I could eat you!" Yet all the time it was me she was looking at. I gave a start, unable to hide my alarm.

Then all those long-toothed people with livid faces began to hoot with laughter.

Old Chen hurried forward and dragged me home.

. . . .

A few days ago a tenant of ours from Wolf Cub village came to report the failure of the crops and told my elder brother that a notorious character in their village had been beaten to death; then *some people had taken out his heart and liver, fried them in oil, and eaten them* as a means of increasing their courage.

When I interrupted, the tenant and my brother both stared at me. Only today have I realized that they had exactly the same look in their eyes as those people outside. Just to think of it set me shivering from the crown of my head to the soles of my feet.

They eat human beings, so they may eat me.

I see that the woman's *"eat you,"* the laughter of those long toothed people with livid faces, and the tenant's story the other day are obviously secret signs. I realize all the poison in their speech, all the daggers in their laughter. Their teeth are white and glistening; *they use these teeth to eat men.*

Evidently, although I am not a bad man, ever since I trod on Mr. Gu's[1] ledgers it has been touch-and-go with me. They seem to have secrets I cannot guess. . . . How can I possibly guess their secret thought--especially when *they are ready to eat people*?

Everything requires careful consideration if one is to understand it. In ancient times, as I recollect, *people often ate human beings*, but I am rather hazy about it.

I tried to look this up but my history book has no chronology and scrawled all over each page are the words " Confucian Virtue and Morality." Since I could not sleep anyway, I read intently half of the night until I began to see words between the lines. The whole book was filled with the two words: *"eat people."*

. . .

I too am a man, and *they want to eat me*!

IV

In the morning I sat quietly for some time. Old Chen brought in lunch: one bowl of vegetables, one bowl of steamed fish. The eyes of the fish were white and hard, and its mouth was open just like those people who want to eat human beings. After a few mouthfuls, I could not tell whether the slippery morsels were fish or human flesh, so I brought it all up.

I said, "Old Chen, tell my brother that I feel quite suffocated . ."
[Then his brother came in and said].
" I have invited Mr. Ho here to today to examine you."
"All right," I replied. Actually, I knew quite well that his old man was the executioner in disguise! Feeling my pulse was simply a pretext for him to see how fat I was; for this would *entitle him to a share of my flesh*. Still I was not afraid. Although I do not eat men my courage is greater than theirs. I held out my two fists to see what he would do. The old man sat down, closed his eyes, fumbled for some time, remained motionless for a while; then opened his shifty eyes and said, "Don't let your imagination run away with you. Rest quietly for a few days, and you will be better.

Don't let your imagination run away with you! Rest quietly for a few days! *By fattening me of course they'll have more to eat.* But what good will it do me?

How can it be "better"? The whole lot of them *wanting to eat people* yet stealthily trying to keep up appearance, not daring to do it outright, was really enough to make me die of laughter. I couldn't help it, I nearly split my sides, and I was so amused. I knew that his laughter voiced courage and integrity. Both the old man and my brother turned pale, awed by my courage and integrity.

But *my courage just makes them all the more eager to eat me*, to acquire some of my courage for themselves. The old man went out of the gate but before he had gone far he said to my brother in a low voice, "To be eaten at once!" My brother nodded. So you are in it too! This stupendous discovery, though it came as a shock, is no more than I might expect: the accomplice *in eating me* is my elder brother!

The eater of human flesh is my elder brother!

I am *the younger brother of an eater of human flesh*!

I, *who will be eaten by others, am the youngest brother of an eater of human flesh*!

. . . .

XII

I can't bear to think of it.

It has only just dawned on me that all these years I have been living in a place where for four thousand years human flesh has been eaten. My brother had just taken over the charge of the house *when our sister died, and he may* have used her flesh in our food, making us eat it unwittingly.

I may have eaten several pieces of my sister's flesh unwittingly, and now it is my turn . . .

How can a man like myself, after four thousand years *of man-eating* history—even though I knew nothing about it at first—ever hope to face real men?

XIII
Perhaps there are still children *who haven't eaten men*?
Save the children...
April 2, 1908 (Italics added, *Lu Xun*, pp. 3-12).

A radical revolutionary writer in the first few decades of the 1900s, Lu Xun was famous for using writing as a weapon to awaken the Chinese people and to call on them to fight social injustice, then rampant in society, and to destroy the feudalist system and the oppressive traditional Chinese culture. He wrote this story in 1908, three years before the collapse of the Qing Dynasy and the overthrow of the last emperor in China. With this background in mind, it is thus clear for us to see that in this story, Lu Xun is depicting an insane society via the eyes of a "demented man." He very effectively achieves his goal by comparing, to the eating of human beings, the inhuman oppression of the Chinese people by the ruling class and by the traditional feudal morality and customs epitomized in some of the Confucian teachings. The Chinese state apparatus and its social structure from ancient to present are compared to a cannibal human creature devouring every single member of the society. That is why the "madman" discovered that the whole history book he was reading "was filled with the two words: 'eat people'" despite the fact that the words of Confucian morality and righteousness were written all over the book "After four thousand years of man-eating history," this hypocritical society has destroyed humanity, leaving the "madman" wondering how he can "ever hope to face real men." It is necessary to point out here that "A Madman's Diary" is not Lu Xun's only work where the man-eating metaphor is used. His "Writing under the Lamp" and "Grave Epitaph" are essays where the man-eating metaphor also serves to condemn the traditional morals and creeds. More importantly, Lu Xun was not the only author in the early twentieth century to employ the eating metaphor to castigate the corrupt and decadent society and the hypocritical aspects of traditional Chinese culture. So did Wu Yu in "*Chiren Yu Lijiao*" ("Man-eating and Moral Creeds]" and Zhou Zuoren in "*Chi Lieshi*" ("Eating Martyrs.")

In fact, according to Liu Zaifu and Lin Gan (1988), two renowned Chinese contemporary literary critics, denouncing this "man-eating banquet" is a major literary and political theme of the May 4th movement. Liu Zaifu and Lin Gan devoted to the topic a whole book chapter entitled "The discovery of 'man-eating' feast." They called many of the writers of the May 4th movement "sweepers of the street of thought" and claimed that "these sweepers are laboring conscientiously, trying to sweep away thousands of years of cumulated garbage. What are the first cultural dregs that they try to get rid of? The answer is, to using the popular language of the time, '*the man-eating feast*'" (Liu Zaifu and Lin Gan, 1988, p. 101). In summarizing how the May 4th writers expose and condemn the evils of the society and cultural traditions, Liu Zaifu and Lin Gan (1988, p. 102) write,

> The May 4th era writers render a thorough portrayal and condemnation of the various types of "man-eating" committed by the established "spiritual civilization." In general, there are three types. First, man-eating--the ruling-class cannibals eat others. From the top onto the bottom, the rulers carry out cruel oppression of the people under them. Second, man-eating--those who themselves are being eaten eat others. These individuals are on the one hand being oppressed but they are simultaneously oppressing those who are weaker than them, i.e. while they are being devoured, they are devouring others who are weaker than them. They are what Lu Xun described in "A Madman's Diary" as the "I-eat-men-too" individuals. Thirdly, man-eating--self-eating. These are the people who totally oppress their own ego and destroy themselves in the process. This self-destruction man-eating is the most deplorable and horrible type of Chinese "men-eating." Although there are different types of "men-eating," their basic goal is the same: eliminating human beings and turn them into "slaves" or "masters."

The practice of using metaphor to condemn social evils is still popular today. A commentary that Lin Chuangcheng (1996) wrote in *Shijie Ribao* provides a good example. Lin was criticizing Wuhan (a large city in central China) Municipal Government's policy of fining women who were found non-virgins at their pre-marriage physical examination, and he did so by writing sarcastically in the Municipal Government's voice to defend such a policy. The title of the commentary is "Tyrannical Government Eats Non-virgins." After stating sarcastically there was nothing wrong in the policy, he concluded his piece by stating, "It has been thirty years since the Cultural Revolution. Confucianism proves to be undefeatable. Since Confucianism can eat people, why cannot a tyrannical government eat non-virgins?" (Lin Chuangcheng, 1996, p. B10). Lin's remark that "Confucianism can eat people" is a clear reference to Lu Xun's "A madman's diary." It is obvious that the human-eating metaphor has become a well-established literary device in the Chinese language for castigating social evils. There are, of course, many other eating metaphors that are widely used to depict corruptive and decadent behaviors in China. For example, the well-known sarcastic doggerel in China today that is cited as an epigraph at the beginning of the chapter reads "Dagaimao, chileyuangao chibeigao (Chinese judicial professionals such as judges, prosecutors, and police [referred to by the synecdoche: the big cap they all wear] eat their plaintiff first and then eat the defendant)" (Fan Fu, 1996, p. S7). The doggerel satirizes and condemns the judicial officers who take advantages of both the plaintiff (often a victim) and the defendant (often an accused criminal).

What needs to be further pointed out is that in reality, Chinese judicial professionals often do indirectly eat their plaintiffs and defendants—they eat meals with the latter at the latter's expense. An article in *Guangzhou Riba [Daily]* reports the following:

> Shunde [the name of a city]: Officers not allowed to eat the people involved in the case. The People's Court of *Shunde* city strictly follows rules and disciplines in conducting court procedures and has recently decided that case officers must not let people involved in the case pay for the officers' meals and other living expenses. The court wants to completely solve the problem of the people involved in a case paying for case officers' meals, hotel expenses—a practice that has had sever negative impact on the judicial justice" ("*Shunde*," 2000).

Another popular doggerel in China denouncing government officials' corruption is "*liangtou chi, chi liangtou*" ["two heads eat ; eat two ends"] (cited from Wang Luowang, 1996, p. S3). It derides many officials' scheme of "eating the fat meat of the state-owned business." The scheme involves 1) listing family members or relatives as ghost employees of the state-owned business where the official works, hence "two heads (the official and his family members) eating the 'fat meat,'" and 2) having the business reimburse all the extravagant personal expenses that were already paid by bribing individuals or private business, thus "eating two ends." There is also the age-old metaphor: "*chi (nuren de) doufu*" ["eat (a woman's) tofu"], meaning to make an advance towards a woman. Today, from this metaphor have derived many disgusting ones that reveal how some immoral men treat women as food for them to enjoy. For example, a report in *Zhongguo Qinnian Bao [Chinese Youth Daily]* quotes a popular saying in Southern China:

"A wife is salted fish—it can be tasted whenever you want; a sister-in-law is a goldfish—it can only be watched but not touched; a street prostitute is grass carp—it tastes good and is also inexpensive" ("Luyou tuan," 2000).

Like family metaphor, eating metaphor has also found its way into the discussion of the relationship between Beijing and Taiwan. Many in Taiwan do not want to discuss unification with Beijing because they are afraid that unification will end in Beijing's *chi diao* (literally "eating up") Taiwan. To dispel this fear by Taiwan, Beijing's leaders have repeatedly stated that Beijing will not *eat up* Taiwan in the process of unification. For example, in a speech to a delegation of overseas Chinese from America, Deng Xiaoping (1983) asserted, "Peaceful unification [of Mainland China and Taiwan] is the consensus of the two Parties [the Communist Party in the Mainland and the Nationalist Party in Taiwan]. Such unification does not mean *I eat up you* or *you eat up me*" and for emphasis, Deng reiterated the point again later in the speech "Peaceful unification does not mean that the *Mainland eats up Taiwan*, nor, of course, does it mean that *Taiwan eats up the Mainland*" (Vol. 3, pp. 30-31). Similarly, Qian Qichen, China's current Vice Premier in charge of foreign affairs and Taiwan issues, also told a delegation from Taiwan that "People on both sides [of the Taiwan Strait] are Chinese, so there is no such an issue of *who is eating up who*" ("Qian Qichen: Liangan doushi zhongguo," 2000). Many overseas Chinese who support the unification of Beijing and Taiwan also joined the force to dismiss the fear. Pan Yazhong, Chairman of the World Chinese Economic Association, was quoted saying at a conference conducted by Chinese Americans in the Eastern U.S. that "many Taiwanese people do not understand what the "one country, two systems" policy is and are afraid that unification means being *eaten up* by the Mainland. In fact, neither the Mainland nor Taiwan can eat up the other" ("Shixian zhongguo tongyi," 2000).

Now let us turn to another Chinese eating metaphor: *chi an* ("eat cases"). The metaphor refers to a common police practice that should be unsettling to the public. It has appeared in many media reports and news commentaries. The title and the lead of an article in Taiwan's *Zhongguo Shibao* (*China Times*) cited below highlight the use of this metaphor.

> "*Chi an*: A series of police eating cases—*Eating cases* both the hard way and the soft way."

(April 23, 1999) Not a few front-line police officers modestly claim that *eating cases* is a very important part of police work. Most of those who have worked in the criminal division of local police stations or branches all have had this experience [eating cases]. Their skills in eating cases vary considerably with some being profoundly experienced and some not so experienced. If you *eat[cases]* beautifully, there will be less pressure from your superiors and they will be more appreciated and even awarded. Yet sometimes, you find yourself having great trouble *swallowing [cases]* but you have to force yourself to *swallow them]*. You also have to *swallow into your stomach* the bitterness and hardships involved in *eating cases*. It doesn't matter whether *the way you eat* looks good or ugly. The goal of *eating cases* is to make your superior look and feel good and to make yourself look and feel good. (Italics added; "Chi An,"1999)

For Chinese readers, the piece is not difficult at all to comprehend but for non-Chinese readers it can be rather puzzling because of the lack of socio-cultural and language background. For weeks during April and May of 1999, "eating cases" was a major story in Taiwan's media, and all three branches of the government launched an investigation into the matter. What is meant by "eating cases"? Eating cases refers to the police practice of suppressing or under-reporting criminal cases in order to make their policing job appear better than it actually is. Like anything that has been eaten, when a case is eaten, it disappears from sight. Also, like the way any food can be eaten, there are different ways, according to the report, to eat--suppress or under-report--cases. Skillfully suppressing or under-reporting cases is "eating [cases] beautifully." Cases that are difficult to suppress or under-report often make police officers have "great trouble swallowing" them. Yet whatever way you suppress or under-report a case, whether looking "good or ugly", the purpose remains the same--to make your superior and yourself do less work but appear better in terms of job performance.

Suppressing/under-reporting cases has not been the only police practice that has been compared to eating. So has the practice of taking advantage of victims and the accused, as pointed out earlier in the example of the doggerel of judicial officers eating the plaintiff first and then eating the defendant. It is no accident that Chinese enjoying using the eating metaphor to criticize corruptions and vice in society. Chinese people have an unusual passion for eating. Furthermore, in Chinese culture, the state and the family are conflated, making it easy for Chinese speakers to view social problems in terms of familiar activities in the home, on the dining table in this particular case. The plaintiff/defendant-eating judicial officers, the virgin-eating municipal government, and the man-eating society all make perfect sense in this cultural context. In short, while in American English, as shown previously, one can "play," "sell," and "buy" almost anything, in the Chinese language, one can eat almost anything. In a way, citizens' lives, as Wang Jun(2001) puts it in his article about the relationship between cooking and governing a country, "are like eating in a restaurant."

A look at the first few paragraphs of Jun Wang's essay will help us understand how governing is like cooking and how citizen's daily lives are similar to eating in a restaurant:

> Lao Zi [also known as Lao Tzu] says, "Ruling a large country is like cooking a delicacy dish." On the one hand, the statement appears to mean that governing a country is not too difficult a task; on the other hand, it seems to suggest that governing a county is a very delicate matter. If it is well done, the delicacy has a great tenderness, an enticing fragrance, and a wonderful taste. Yet if done wrong, the dish is a pile of messy burned tiny pieces of meat and vegetables, greatly damaging the name of the chef.
>
> In fact, governing a country is like cooking a dish. Citizens' normal lives are like going to and eating in a restaurant. If the restaurant has a good reputation, diners all want to frequent it. They sit down, sip tea and order dishes. Chefs get busy cooking, and then delicious dishes are served. The clients are content and happy. So are the restaurant owner and the employees. The clients come back again and again. The chef becomes famous and the restaurant well known, full of life and full of happiness.
>
> Yet what will and can you do if a restaurant's management is a mean bully, coercing you into the restaurant, tying you to a seat, and forcing food and drink down your throat, and if the chef, regardless of your taste, cooks a big mixed pot hated by all that contains fake fish, rotten meat, pig hair, and vegetables with mud? You want to leave but you can't, and you don't want eat but you have to because the restaurant will starve you for three days. From the fourth day on, you will be very hungry and will close your eyes and swallow down whatever to fill your empty stomach. After many years, you will not be able to tell what a real good life is like. What is worse, you may take these thieves as your parents and assist them in their evil deeds.
>
> Or what will it be like if a restaurant has an excellent reputation but a bad client walks in, sits down, when given the menu, throws it away, walks into the kitchen, forces out the chef, and tries to cook himself? If

this mean client knows how to cook, it may not be too bad as he can feed himself although he will surely discourage the other clients. If he does not know how to cook, things will be much worse as he hurts both himself and the other clients and ruins the restaurant's business. What is worse, if this wicked client yelled at all the other clients to come into the kitchen to cook for themselves. There will be no more rules, no more order, no more art of cooking, and no more civilization.

Therefore, it is clear if the clients are good and the restaurant's owner is nice, everything will be peaceful; if the clients are mean and the owner is evil, an upheaval will ensue.

Wang Jun then goes on in the essay to compare contemporary China to the latter scenario where some wicked citizens (restaurant clients) fight with a mean government (restaurant owner). He concludes the essay stating, "Lao Zi says, `Ruling a large country is like cooking a delicacy dish.' In this world, big and important things may be understood from something small. Whether it is managing a county or cooking a dish, the result is determined by the morality and behavior of the restaurant's clients and the owner; whether the world will be in peace or upheaval is decided by the people's behavior, mentality, and morality." Via the restaurant eating metaphor, Wang Junrenders, to the Chinese people, a clear and easy-to-understand argument that a prosperous and peaceful country can only be achieved by the joined efforts of both moral citizens (restaurant diners) and a benevolent government (restaurant owner).

Chinese people's tendency to view life events as eating could perhaps best been seen in several media commentaries about the 2002 Chinese Central TV's *chun jie wang hui* (New Year's Eve Show), a medley of various types of entertainment including, among other things, singing, dancing, and comedy shows. Like the Super Bowl in U.S., this medley show has been the mostly watched entertainment TV program in China since its commencement in the late 1970s. In recent years, because of the audience's increased expectations and because of the organizers' difficulty in coming up with new items that would appeal to the entire audience, the program has received some severe criticism. The 2002 program was no exception. Of the critical commentaries I read, quite a few in their criticism treated the TV entertainment show as a food party. One entitled "Chunjie wanhui zhe dao cai zhende shou le ma [Has the New Year's Eve Party Show really gone sour/bad]" reads:

(Chinesenewsnet, 2/12/2002). Some say that the New Year's Eve

Show has become a brand name of Chinese entertainment industry and an indispensable New Year's Eve's *feast* to the Chinese people. Others aay the show has become such a routine of old stuff that it *tastes bland*; it's a waste of effort and money and it should be completely overhauled—the opposite voices started filling our ears several years ago. This year the latter voice seems to have gained more support. Although this year's Near Year's Eve Show was coherent, lively, warm, and jubilant, not a single item left the audience with a relatively deep impression. So even while the show was still going on, criticism already appeared on the internet, making us wonder: Has the New Year's Eve Show dish really gone sour?

The author then goes on to criticize the various problems with the show and then points out that many provincial TV stations have began to produce their own New Year's Eve shows so as to, in the author's words, "*get a cup of the soup*" from the show meal. The author concludes, "with an increasing competition among different media modes and organizations, the time is not too far away when each TV station makes its own *New Year's Eve meal*."

Also using the eating metaphor, another commentary entitled "Chunjie lianhuan wanhui ha zhong qu chong, fenshi taiping [The New Year's Eve Show: A claptrap attempting to paint a rosy picture]" (2/14, 2002) begins its attack on the show by saying: "Every year, with the invasion of commercialism and the addition of *strong spices* by the producer/director and media, the Chinese Central TV's New Year's Eve Show has grown clumsily huge, like a large fat guy with a big potbelly who has *eaten too much fat*." After discussing some of the problems in the show, the author states, "the unfortunate 1.2 billion Chinese, faced with this accustomed *New Year's Eve meal*, are bombarded by the *instant-noodle-like program items*." The author attributes the failure of the show to the Chinese Central TV's superficial effort "to be audience's *wine and meat friends* who *eat, drink,* and party to have fun. . ." and faults the station for not trying to be audience's true confidant by showing the audience truth and talking to them heart to heart. In the two critics' mind, this Chinese Central TV medley show is truly a dish that has gone bad.

All the above discussion has shown the extensive use of the eating metaphor in the Chinese language. There are numerous instances where actions or events in China are viewed in terms of eating. For more examples, see the Glossary of Dominant Metaphorical Idioms at the end of the book.

Notes

1. Mr. Gu here refers to Gu Jiu, a fictitious name meaning "old" used as an allegory standing for the age-old history of feudalism in China.

Chapter 9

Spinning Wheels in English and *Singing Red and White Faces* in Chinese: More Examples of Culture-specific Metaphors

Thus far, I have demonstrated how sports and business form two dominant metaphors in American English (Chapters 2 to 5) and how family and eating manage to be two prominent sources for metaphors in the Chinese language (Chapters 6 to 8). In this chapter, I plan to further illustrate the culture-specific nature of metaphor by introducing and exploring the use of driving metaphor in American English and the use of Beijing opera/acting metaphor in Chinese. While it is true that either metaphor is used in both languages, any close examination and comparison will show that driving metaphor is far more extensively used in American English than in Chinese, and the opposite is true of the opera/acting metaphor. Such metaphor use, I assert, is the product of popular cultural practices in the two countries respectively.

Let us first look at the use of driving-related metaphors in American English. It is a well-known fact that America is the birthplace and a kingdom of automobiles. It is a country that not only enjoys the largest overall number of automobiles in the world but also boasts one of world's highest, if not the highest, rate of car ownership per capita. The majority of Americans have access to an automobile and almost all Americans over the legal driving age know how to drive. This easy access to automobiles has led the American public to a high familiarity with and a decent knowledge of automobiles and driving, a knowledge that not many people in the rest of world have the luxury of possessing.

The American public's good knowledge about driving has in turn resulted in their ability and urge, whether conscious or unconscious, to use driving related metaphors to describe human behavior and experience in a unique and effective fashion that other metaphors or other means may not be able to provide. The images that these driving metaphors offer about the relevant human behaviors and experience are often very accurate and extremely vivid.

For example, to begin or become prepared for something is to *crank up* or *get cranked up*--the way a car is started. If something (or someone) is the driving force in an activity, then it is said to be *the engine* of the action. To take the lead or play the leading role in an activity or an event is to *take* (or *be in*) *the driver's seat*, an image that best captures the nature of what the person is doing. It is no wonder during election campaigns we often hear the comment about a candidate *being in the driver's seat* when he/she is leading in the poll by a large margin. By the same token, the expression, to *take* or *be in the backseat*, also accurately presents the picture of someone playing a very passive role in an event. Similarly, there is perhaps no better metaphorical expression than that of the *backseat driver* in depicting the annoying person who stands by with regard to an action but keeps giving commands about how to conduct it. Many other driving metaphors are equally expressive. To change a topic in a conversation or to change an item in the agenda of an ongoing event is indeed not very much different from *shifting* or *switching gears* in the process of driving. To augment the intensity of an activity is surely very much like *going up a gear*. Furthermore, to achieve the goal of augmenting the intensity and *going up a gear* in the activity, a person certainly will need to *step on it* (the accelerator), i.e. to increase one's effort. When the activity reaches high intensity, then it is said, in a vivid way, to *be in high gear*, running with full power and speed. Furthermore, if one is exerting a lot of effort in doing something but is accomplishing little or nothing, the person is rightly deemed to be *spinning wheels*, and will likely be asked to *put brakes on it*--to stop it.

A driving metaphor that is quite opposite of *spinning wheels* is *gaining a lot of mileage by doing* (or *from/out of*) *something* because when a person is said to have gained a lot of mileage in doing something, it means that the individual has maximized the return of his effort by making a right move or doing something effectively or smartly. When all the departments or members of an organization are working cooperatively and functioning smoothly in accomplishing the organization's goals and objectives, the organization is believed to *be running with all six* (or *eight*) cylinders. However, if some departments or members are not functioning, the institution is deemed to be operating *without all its cylinders running*. When things are not running well at a place, it is time to *grease the wheels* so as to make them operate more efficiently and smoothly. Yet sometimes actions taken may have the opposite effect and such actions are said to have *backfired* as car engines sometimes do. Of course, there is also the well-known expression "to *give the green light to somebody or something,*" one that conveys perhaps better than any other expressions the meaning of issuing the go-ahead signal for someone or something. Such is also the case with the metaphor *"making a U turn."* It renders the complete turn-about of a person's decision or opinion in a mental image that is so easy to picture and comprehend. The same may also be said of the driving metaphors such as living *in the fast lane*, meaning living a busy or recklessly hedonistic life depending on the types of life the depicted person is living. A very important point about all these driving metaphors is that they are all everyday colloquial expressions, a fact that further testifies to their popularity.

Beijing opera, formerly known as Peking opera, is a traditional opera-play that involves both stage singing and acting/fighting. Although it is no longer as popular as it used to be (especially with today's youth), Beijing opera is still considered China's national opera/play because of its significant place in Chinese culture. Born in Beijing, the capital of China for almost all of the past 600 years, Beijing opera has historically been a major form of entertainment for the ruling class as well as for the general public in the cities.[1] Until the height of market economic reform in the 1990s, there had been a Beijing opera troupe not only in every province but also in almost all big and mid-sized cities in China. Beijing opera was made especially well-known and popular during the Cultural Revolution (1966-1976) when the government allowed basically only eight plays to be performed. The eight plays are known as the Eight Revolutionary Model Plays designated by Chairman Mao Zedong's wife Jiang Qing. Of these eight plays, all, except for two ballets, are Beijing operas.[2] These operas were also all made into stage movies for the entire population to watch at that time. Furthermore, troupes of local (non-Beijing) operas were also encouraged to show adapted versions of the model plays. Given that the Cultural Revolution era was a time with no TV and few other entertainment venues, these model plays were the most common, if not the only, visual entertainment for most Chinese.

The importance of the Beijing opera or other Chinese operas in the Chinese language, for that matter, is the fact that while in English, an actor *plays* a role in a drama, movie or play, an actor in Chinese *chang* (*sings*) a role. A by-product of the popularity of Beijing opera across the country and the popularity of the local operas and plays in their own regions is the use of metaphors based on Beijing opera and acting performance in general. For example, in the traditional Beijing opera, a character with a red made-up face is a moral and virtuous person or a "good guy" in plain English, but a character with a white made-up face is a wicked and base individual or a "bad guy." Hence the expression "one sings the red face and the other sings the white face" is the Chinese equivalent of the English expression "one plays the good/nice guy and the other plays the bad guy" in business dealings or other engagements. To play a very minor or supporting role in Beijing opera is *pao longtao* [*pao* means "run" and *longtao* means the outfit worn by ancient imperial guards so the whole phrase means "run across the stage in a guard's outfit"]. This jargon is now widely used to refer to playing a supporting or insignificant role.

A somewhat related expression is *zou guochang* [walk through the stage] meaning to do something superficially for the purpose of creating the impression of doing the work. In Beijing opera, the main character often either sings a solo or a duet with his or her antagonist. To sing a solo is called *chang dujiao xi*, an expression now frequently employed to mean, negatively, that a person is alone without any support in an activity. To give an opposing duet is to *chang duitai xi*. When one *chang duitai xi* against another person or organization, it means to take a position against the other person by doing or saying the opposite of what the latter is doing or saying. Of course, it can also mean simply to try to compete with or rival the latter. For example, recently China has been reported to like to *chang duitai xi* against the U.S. on many international issues. Another term from Beijing opera that has been widely used metaphorically is *jinluo migu*—meaning to beat gongs and drums with an increasing speed and loudness. In Beijing opera, beating gongs and drums faster and faster and louder and louder signals the imminent raising of the curtain or the beginning of an important action. It has been used figuratively to refer to an intense publicity campaign that harbingers the imminent undertaking of an important cause/action/policy. For instance, the then U.S. Secretary of Defense

Dick Cheney's visit to several Middle East nations before the Gulf War in 1991 could be said to be part of a series of *jinluo migu* for the start of the war.

The popular use of opera metaphor in Chinese can be seen in the following excerpt from a recent Chinese TV movie series entitled *Breaking Silence* (2001). The movie series centers around corruption problems in today's China. Two of the main characters in the movie are Mayor Zhao, the mayor of a big city, and Tang Jinzhou, the CEO of the largest stockbrokerage firm in the same city. The two are colluding in various money schemes and frauds but each has a different agenda. The following are exchanges between the two after Tang heard that the mayor launched a severe attack on the City's Communist Party Secretary, who is expected to be Tang's future mother-in-law, at the municipal Party's Standing Committee (the highest power in the city).

> *Zhao*: How come you came here? Are you tired of counting money.
> *Tang*: Mayor Zhao, I heard that your *acting* at the Party Standing Committee was sensational.
> *Zhao*: On whose behalf are you making the accusation? On behalf of our good Party Secretary or your future mother-in-law?
> *Tang*: I'm here just to ask you whether it was really necessary for you to come out in such a hurry and put on this *bigong xi* [*bi gong* opera, referring to the act in historical operas where ministers tried to force the emperor to abdicate].
> *Zhao*: Hurry? Hum! If I don't strike now, I may not even have the chance to hurry in the future . . . [The mayor goes on to shout out why he has to act now]. [Then the mayor continues] Don't try to pressure me on any thing. I hope you're not here to pressure me.
> *Tang*: I'm here simply to ask you not to cause trouble. Our *opera is half sung. Better episodes are yet to come.* You don't need to make everyone extremely nervous and unhappy.
> *Zhao*: Well said. Then I'll wait to *listen to your better episodes.* When you *finish singing the opera,* you can then leave and go far away. As for my business, you don't need to worry anymore.
> *Tang*: Don't forget. The *remaining opera needs me to sing.*
> *Zhao*: Isn't it for the purpose of *singing this opera well* that you have raised so much money from various channels? *Don't you dare not to sing it now.* Don't act emotionally for a woman [the Party Secretary's daughter]. It isn't the right attitude and style for a financier.

It is clear here that both characters view themselves as opera singers and see what they are doing as singing performance. More importantly, the whole dialogue is threaded together, seamlessly I would like to add, by opera singing metaphors. It certainly requires an audience familiar with the metaphors for the dialogue to work. The Chinese public provides such an audience.

Besides these metaphors that are known to have come directly from Beijing opera, there are many other frequently used opera/play metaphors in Chinese. For example, to take over a position or to be in power, especially at the national level, is *deng tai* or *shang tai* [to mount a stage] whereas to step down from a position or to be out of power is *xia tai* [step down from a stage]. There is basically no other way of expressing the ideas in Chinese. A leader is thus compared to a stage actor, and running a nation or an institution is tantamount to rendering a stage performance. Cao Changqing's (2001) political commentary about the differences between Russian President Putin's and Chinese President Jiang Zemin's performances on the world stage highlights the use of this Chinese metaphor. Concerning the two leaders' responses to the September 11, 2001 attack on the U.S., Cao Changqing argues that Putin gave a much better performance than Jiang. He then went on to explain why Putin outperformed Jiang:

> Of course, both Putin's and Jiang's actions were to a certain degree political *shows*. Yet even so, why did Putin *perform* beautifully? The key is that Russia has now become a democracy. Putin *shang tai* ("got on the stage") through election. If he does not try to maintain the support of the people, he may lose out in the next election. In today's Russia, it is the *audience* and the ballots the *audience* hold that will judge Putin's *show*, evaluating his *performance* level and determining his future political fate. Putin has to be humble, work hard, behave appropriately, and pay attention to and respect public opinions and media coverage.
>
> Yet it is different in China. While Jiang Zemin is also a *protagonist on the stage*, it is not for the *audience* to assess and determine how he *performs* and whether he has the ability to *perform*. Moreover, if anyone in the *audience* dares not to laud, flatter, and sycophantize Jiang's *performance*, he/she will be removed from the *show* or even be arrested and sentenced.
> ...
> For Putin, it is the audience who decide his fate but for Jiang, it is he who determines the fate of *the audience*. That is the biggest difference between today's China and Russia, and that is also the greatest difference between Jiang and Putin. (Cao Changqing, 2001).

Whether a Chinese reader agrees with Cao Changqing's assessment and criticism of Jiang, the use of the acting metaphor certainly strikes a cord.

There are also several opera/play metaphors that contain the Chinese word "*xi*," which may mean either an opera or a play. When there is no hope for winning something or for attaining a goal, etc., Chinese like to say *mei xi changle* or simply *mei xi le* [having no more opera to sing], meaning it is over. The opposite is *you xi changle* or *you xi chang* [having opera to sing], which implies that there is still a lot to be played out and determined or there is still a lot of hope. If someone is not serious in doing or saying something but merely doing it to please the people present, he or she is said to *fengchang zuoxi* [to render an impromptu performance according to the occasion]. Of course, a person who does it will not be well received when found out. If a task or an accomplishment is easy, commonplace, or trivial, it is often called *er xi*, meaning literally "children's play." Another interesting acting metaphor is *chang* [sing] *shuanghuang*. *Shuanghuang* is a unique Chinese stage performance where two actors cooperate seamlessly to make it appear as if only one person is giving the performance. During the performance, one actor hides behind the other and is chiefly responsible for providing the vocal performance whereas the front actor does most of the physical actions. The phrase *chang shuanghuang* [sing double voice] has been a popular metaphor used to describe two individuals who stage a scheme to cheat others. One more *xi* related metaphor is *yazhou xi* [the last act of an opera]. It is used to mean the last but most important item in the agenda of an activity such as a meeting. Thus, to conduct or present the last but perhaps the most important item in an event is *chang yazhou xi* [sing the last act of an opera].

Of course, there are also those common and easy to understand acting/singing metaphors: *chang fan diao* [sing an opposite tune], meaning to say and do the opposite; *chang gao diao* [sing a high tune], meaning to take a high moral ground in order to make oneself appear more courageous, more moral, or more honorable than one actually is so as to place one's opponents in a less favorable and less comfortable position; *chang* (or *bao chi*) *di diao*[sing or keep a low tune], meaning to act quietly not so as not to draw attention to oneself, or to keep a low profile as English speakers would say. These singing metaphors are used very frequently. For example, the last of the three, *chang di diao*, was employed extensively in all Chinese language media including those in America, China, Hong Kong, and Taiwan in portraying Chinese Vice President Hu Jintao during his recent visit to the U.S. in late April and early May, 2002. He was repeatedly called a master of *di diao* and was said to have done a great job in keeping "a low tune" to ensure his chance of succeeding Jiang Zemin as China's next leader. As commentator Ba Dun (2002), writes in his article "Low tune is better than high tune for Hu Jintao,"

> Chinese Vice President Hu Jintao is currently on an official trip that includes the visit, in turn, of Malaysia, Singapore, and the U.S. Before the trip and now during the trip, many political commentators and reporters around the world have been making various remarks about Hu. The term *"low tune"* has appeared very frequently in these comments. Using the same term, all of them commented on Vice President Hu's *low tune* in dealing with people and handling things. This *"low tune"* seems to contain a little negative meaning. Many don't realize that, for a politician, *low tune* in handling things has, since ancient times, always been better than *high tune*.

Then Ba Dun goes on to discuss how political leaders' *high tune* has led to many disasters in recent Chinese history including the "Great Leap Forward" movement and the Cultural Revolution, the former an overly bold and unrealistic economic and production drive launched by Mao Zedong in the late 1950s that ended with the starvation and death of millions of people, and the latter a political movement (1966-1976) also started by Mao that brought China political and economic havoc. Ba Dun then explains what *"low tune"* means: *"Low tune* means being truthful, kind and easy to get along, modest. . ." In conclusion, Ba Dun argues,

> In my opinion, *low tune* is better than *hi tune*. Why has Hu Jintao already received so many praises in just the first leg [Malaysia] of his trip? It is because he is open-minded, modest, earnest, and *low tune* in handling every thing. He shows no airs and does not endorse glorification and publicity for himself. He is only interested in conducting everything right and well. He does not possess the haughtiness that often characterizes leaders of big counties nor does he have the meekness that some leaders of developing counties tend to show. He is well-received wherever he visits. It is not that Hu cannot be *hight tune*; it is because he doesn't want to.

Of course, critics would contend that Hu really does not dare to sing a *high tune* before he takes over the leadership because he knows that in the recent Chinese history several designated leaders-to-be were ousted because of their *high tune* behavior including Hu Yaobang and Zhao Ziyang, both of whom were Deng Xiaoping's protégés but both were purged by him for not following his policies closely.

In China, it is not just political leaders who are considered performers in carrying out their important responsibilities. As already shown above in the example from the excerpt of the Chinese TV movie series *Breaking Silence*, even ordinary citizens in doing their daily functions are also viewed as performers. An additional example is the age-old acting-related metaphorical expression *fuchang fusui*, whose literal translation is "What a husband sings, the wife follows." Reflecting a very sexist traditional belief, the expression means that in a family, the wife should play only a supporting role for her husband, doing and saying whatever her husband does and says. Thus in Chinese, even people as mundane as a married-couple are seen as actors, although in this case a duet that is supposed to be sung in only one tune. Finally, when a person designs and does something as a scheme all by him/herself, the individual is said in Chinese to have *self-directed and self-acted out a mischievous or wicked drama*. All this is not surprising in a culture where a famous saying about life is that *rensheng ru xi*—human life is like a drama!

Notes

1. In addition to Bejing opera, there have been many other local operas in China such as Henan opera, Shaoxing opera, and Guangdong opera. But none of these operas has really spread out of its region and therefore they have all remained largely local operas.

2. The six Model Beijing operas are: Hongdan Ji (The tale of the Red Lamp), Shajia Bang, Zhiqu Weihu Shan, Hai Gang, Qixi Baihu Tuan, and Dujun Shan. These opera names were to the Chinese during the Cultural Revolution as the Christmas Carol is to Americans. Jiang Qing and her followers made some changes to Beijing opera but the changes were mostly in the topics of the plays and costumes that the actors wear. Traditionally, the topics of Beijing opera were mostly about famous past historical events, mainly the stories of the emperors, warriors, and other famous historical figures. The Revolutionary model operas are contemporary stories, often propaganda tales. Despite the changes, these contemporary plays remain true to Beijing opera in terms of the style of singing and fighting characteristic of Beijing opera.

Chapter 10

Drop the Ball vs. *Za Guo Le* [*Breaking the Cooking Pot*]: A Comparison of Cultural Views and Cross-Language Influence in Metaphor Use

This last chapter consists of two parts. In the first part, I will try to highlight the different worldviews of the Americans and the Chinese by juxtaposing some American metaphors with those in Chinese that express the same or similar meanings. In the second part, I will discuss the influence of American English on Chinese and vice versa in terms of the metaphors used by examining some of the metaphors that have crossed over from one language to the other. To help accomplish the first goal, paired American English and Chinese metaphors will be presented to help illustrate that what Americans see in terms of sports, business, and driving is often viewed by Chinese as family matter, eating, acting, etc.

Let us first review the two pairs I mentioned in the introduction chapter. In the case of the English metaphor "cash in" versus the Chinese *lao youshui* [scoop oil water], while both expressions suggest "to take advantage of something or a situation," the former renders the meaning in business terms but the latter in eating. In the case of the English metaphor "call the shots" versus the Chinese figurative expression *dang jia* [manage the family], although both convey the meaning of "to be in control," the English idiom portrays it in terms of sports but the Chinese does it in terms of family. There are many more such contrastive examples. Let us compare some American sports metaphors with some Chinese eating metaphors. Both the English expression "dropped the ball" and the Chinese idiom "*za guo le*" [broke the cooking pot] mean to have failed or made an error in carrying out something, but they communicate the meaning using different analogies—one sports and one eating. Similarly, the American English boxing metaphor "be on the ropes" and the Chinese metaphors "*wonzhong zi bie*" [a turtle in the cooking pot] and "*panzhong zi wu*" [something in a dish] all express the meaning that one is cornered and about to be defeated. Along the same line, the American boxing metaphor "to let someone off when you had him on the ropes" and the Chinese eating metaphor "*rang zhushu de yazi fei le*" [to let the cooked duck fly away] convey exactly the same meaning: to let go of a sure victor or fail to complete an almost finished task. Another pair of an American sports metaphor and a Chinese eating metaphor is "bench player" and *chi xianfan de ren* [literally "individual who eats free rice and doesn't do much"]. Both refer to an individual who is not very useful or does not contribute much to a team or organization.

Also the English expression "fire a person" and the Chinese phrase "*chao mouren de youyu* ["to fry someone as a squid"] or simply *chaodiao mouren* ["to fry someone"] both mean to dismiss a person from an employment. The English metaphorical expression comes from the hunting sports because in this expression, the discharging of a person is compared to the discharging of a gun. The Chinese expression comes from cooking. When you fry squids, the cut-up squid pieces will turn into rolls. In China, employees of a shop or a restaurant traditionally live in the shop or a room provided by the owner. When an employee is fired, the person will have to roll up his/her bedding, like a fried squid piece is rolled, and leave.

Furthermore, even some non-figurative English sports terms are expressed in eating/food metaphor in Chinese. For example, blocking shots in basketball is best known in Chinese as *gai huoguo* ("covering a hot cooking pot set on a dinning table with live fire underneath it"). This Chinese expression suggests that the basketball shot just made can only go the opposite of the intended direction like the heat of the hot pot being forced back by the covering of a lid. An even more interesting contrastive example is the Chinese equivalent of the English saying "Winner takes all": *yingzhe tong chi* ("Winner eats all"). The notion of taking everything being tantamount to eating all is surely typical of the Chinese mindset. The sports versus eating metaphor contrast can also be found in American and Chinese movies. While both American and Chinese movies use sports and eating metaphors, American movies appear more likely to use sports as a key metaphor for exploring human life experiences (e.g. *Hoop Dreams, He got game, Rocky I-V, Rudy, White man cannot jump*) and Chinese movies tend more likely to tap on eating as a metaphor to examine humanity (e.g. *Eat, Drink, man and women, To Live, Wedding Banquet*, to name a few).

All the above examples help illustrate that the activities that Americans like to perceive as sports tend to be viewed by Chinese as eating or, sometimes, as something else. For example, political campaigns are viewed in American English mostly as sports, as shown in the case of calling elections *races*, but they are seen primarily as military actions in Chinese (I am here referring to Taiwan only because Mainland China does not hold the type of free political elections commonly found in the West). Of course, in American English, elections and other political activities are also sometimes compared to wars as evidenced by campaigns being described as "battles," "fights," and "camps". Yet the use of war metaphors is not as prominent in American English as it is in Chinese in Taiwan. For example, while elections in American English are referred to primarily "*races*" in English, they are called exclusively *xuan zhan* (meaning literally "*election wars*") in Taiwan. Political debates there are also constantly termed as *koushui zhang* (saliva wars), political attacks as *firing cannons* or *bombing*, and political groups or camps as "*jun*" ("armies"), for example, the *Green army* (referring to the currently governing party, the Democratic Progressive Party whose Party flag is primarily green) and the *Blue army* (referring to the once long-time governing party, the Nationalist Party, whose flag is noted for its blue color). Even the supporters of a candidate are frequently called X's (the name of the candidate) army such as "Bian army" (supporters of the current president) and "Ma army" (supporters of the present Mayor of Taipei). The use of war metaphors is so extensive that if you pick up a newspaper during an election in Taiwan, you will be bombarded by words of war, all types. More interestingly, some politicians in Taiwan took these metaphorical terms literally by engaging in physical fights in the parliament. The reason for this dominant use of military terms in describing politics in Chinese, I argue, is that, until 1990s in Taiwan when true democratic elections were first implemented, government changes in Chinese history had almost always taken place as a result of wars in which uprising forces, often peasants, overthrew the government by defeating the latter's armies. In other words, who was to govern had always been decided by wars.

Now let us compare some American business metaphors with some Chinese eating metaphors that have comparable meanings. The American business metaphor *"be short changed"* and the Chinese eating metaphors *chi an qui* [eat a hidden loss] or *zhuo le ren jia de xia fan chai* [having been a dish of food for someone] all express the meaning of having been cheated or manipulated by another party. Similarly, the American business metaphor "to get more than you bargained for" and the Chinese eating metaphor *chi buliao, douzhe zhou* [unable to finish the food that one has asked for or has got for oneself so one has to carry it away in his/her lap] both imply that one has asked for or brought on oneself trouble. Some will say here that English also has a similar eating metaphor in the expression "to get more than one can chew." Yet this English metaphor means mostly that one has taken on a job that he/she does not have the ability or time to accomplish. It usually does not carry the meaning of "landing oneself in trouble" as the Chinese metaphor or the English "to get more than one bargained for" does.

Another contrastive pair of metaphors can be found in American English and Chinese in the expression of an disagreement or opposition to a statement or practice by another person. As I pointed out earlier, a typical American expression is "I don't buy that" and the Chinese is, *"wou bu chi li neitao* [I don't eat your practice or your point of view]." One more example of American business metaphor versus a Chinese eating metaphor is the American expression *"to pay for an action"* and the Chinese *"wei mou shi chi kutou"* [to eat bitterness for some thing one did or for some action one took before]. Both mean the same thing: to bring on oneself suffering because of an earlier action. *Han Ying Cidia* [*A Chinese–English Dictionary*] (1980, p. 395), a widely used dictionary in China, for instance, translates *chi kutou* as "pay for" in its sample sentence: "If you turn a deaf ear to the masses criticism, sooner or later you will *chi kutou* (pay for it)." One more contrasting pair can be found in the American English and Chinese expressions regarding educational classes outside the regular curriculum offered to students for additional learning. In English such classes are called *enrichment* (a word with strong business overtone) but in Chinese they are known as *buxi*, a term that has its root in the term *bushi*, meaning a "nourishing diet" that aims to make a person stronger. It is no wonder often when one attends such classes, he/she is said to *jinbu* (take tonic or extremely nutritious food). One final contrasting example is the American "Don't throw out the baby with the bath water" (a non-business metaphor but a common usage, though) vs. the Chinese *yin yi fei shi* (give up eating for fear of choking). Both the American and Chinese idioms mean basically the same thing ("Don't discard a good thing or practice simply because something related to it is wrong") but their sources differ with the Chinese one derived, again, from eating.

Let us now *switch gears* and compare some American driving metaphors with some Chinese Beijing opera/acting metaphors. When a person is playing a leading role in an action or event, he/she is said to *be in the driver's seat* in English but *chang zhujue* [sing the leading role] in Chinese. When people are prepared and ready for something with great enthusiasm and much publicity, the American English metaphor to describe it is *"They're cranked up"* but the Chinese one is *jiluo migu* ("beat gongs and drums fast and loud").

Now let us turn to the second major issue of this chapter: the influence of American English and the Chinese language upon each other in terms of metaphor use, a mutual influence that is on the rise. With a more and more globalized economy, with the ever-increasing international exchanges in business, education, political dialogues, etc., and with the rapid development and breakthroughs in communication technology, communication among nations of the world has reached an unprecedented extent. Such extensive cross-nation communication has not only exposed speakers of different languages to one another's cultures and worldviews but also allowed these cultures to influence one another. One area of these cross-cultural influences is metaphor use where metaphors from one language invade another. Yet because of the inequality in power among the different cultures and some other factors, the cross-language influence in metaphor use has not been one of balance. Instead, it has been mostly a one-way street with the languages of the speakers that have more power heavily influencing the languages whose speakers have less power. Such is the case, I argue, between American English and the Chinese language.

Any close examination of the two languages regarding the use of metaphors borrowed from the other language will show that the number of American English metaphors that have invaded the Chinese language far exceeds that of those Chinese ones that have found their way into English. There appear to be two rather obvious reasons for this imbalance. First, the English language has been the de facto world lingua franca since the colonial ages due to the expansion of the British Empire in the 18th and 19th centuries and then owing to the rapid rise of the United States on the world stage as a superpower in the 20th century. The second and also a related reason is the ever- increasing influence of American culture, technology, and politics on the rest of the world. The following is a very short list of some of the English metaphors that have entered the Chinese language and gained some popularity:

English	Chinese translation
The ball is in your court	*qiu zai ni ne bian*
Has no credit	*mei xingyu*
Sell an idea, etc.	*tu xiao* or *doushou yi zuyi*
Political capital	*zhengzhi ziben*
Liability	*leizhui, fudan* or *fuzhai*
Time is money	*shijian jiu shi jinqian*
Score points (in politics, etc.	*de fen (zai zhengzhi deng fangmian)*

It seems that the ones that have been easily transferred into Chinese are those that express cultural values that have also been transferred. For example, those business metaphors became popular in China only after its economic reform that began at the end of the 1970s.

Because of different cultural values, the transferring of metaphor is not always a simple straightforward process. Sometimes, an imported metaphor is translated into several slightly different expressions to reflect the cultural values and beliefs of the new host language. For example, the American English "to sell (an idea, etc.)" has been translated into two Chinese expressions that are different in connotation: 1) *tui xiao* (meaning "marketing") and 2) *dou shou* (meaning "peddling"). While the former Chinese translation expression is fairly neutral, the second one is very pejorative. It is important to point out that although in English verb "market" is sometimes also used in place of "sell" in the phrase, the difference between the two verbs is largely a formality (with "market" being much more formal than "sell"). In contrast, the distinction between the two Chinese verbs "*tui xiao*" and "*dou shou*" is strictly connotation. In fact, Chinese does have a perfect equivalent word for "sell"—*mai* but it is not used in this context because, I argue, the Chinese, who have historically disparaged individuals engaged in business or trade, do not believe in any neutral selling when it comes to convincing others to accept what one is saying or doing. They are keen on making this positive and negative distinction when it comes to selling in this figurative sense.

While there are quite a few English metaphorical expressions that have entered the everyday Chinese language, the number of Chinese metaphorical expressions that have found their way into English is extremely minuscule, perhaps just a couple. One of them is *kowtow*, meaning to fawn, a figurative meaning that has derived from its literal meaning of "kneel and touching the forehead to the ground as a token of respect and homage," a practice in Chinese tradition for people of a younger general or of a lower class to show respect to those of a older generation or of a higher class. Another example I have found is the name of a famous Chinese cuisine *tang chu* ("sugar vinegar" or commonly translated as "sweet and sour"). In suggesting how Washington should act towards Beijing after the military airplane collision incident near Hainan, China, in April, 2001, and after Beijing expressed support for the fight against world terrorism following the 9/11 attack on the U.S., Winston Lord, former U.S. Ambassador to China and an expert on Sino-American relationships, said that the Bush administration should make "sweet and sour" moves towards China What he meant, according to his elaboration, was something similar to a "carrot and stick" policy, for he wanted Bush, on the one hand, to commend Beijing on her stance on terrorism and to expand economic cooperation with her (the "sweet" part of a dish) and, on the other hand, to be tough with China on issues such as Taiwan and weapon proliferation (the "sour" part of the dish).

Hopefully, the increasing exchanges between the two nations in business, education, science, and technology, among other things, will help correct the imbalance in the inter-lingual influences between the two languages and, as a result, more metaphors from the Chinese language may find their way into American English.

Conclusion

Metaphor, the process of mapping our understanding of one domain, often a common familiar experience, onto another domain of knowledge, frequently an abstract one, is an inherent part of the human conceptual system. It enables us to understand the world in a way that makes best sense to us. Metaphor and culture are thus closely interwoven. Like language in general, the use of metaphors is simultaneously shaped by and shaping the culture in which the language is spoken. In other words, language speakers' use of metaphors is to a great extent influenced by their cultural experience, and in return, metaphors help shape the speakers' construction of reality--their worldviews. The dominant metaphors that the speakers of a language use can provide an excellent window for us to look at the values and beliefs treasured in their culture and the worldviews they hold. Examining and comparing dominant metaphors from two different languages may help further foreground these cultural beliefs and views in a way that cannot be accomplished otherwise.

The eminent use of sports and business metaphors in Americans English explored in this book reflects Americans' view of life as competitive games and business. In contrast, the prominent use of eating and family metaphors in the Chinese language renders us a glimpse of how the Chinese tend to see life as family eating events. Similarly, while Americans like to interpret life experience in terms of driving, a routine daily activity for many Americans, Chinese customarily consider their world an opera stage for them to sing or perform on. Such respective worldviews can also be traced to some cultural models or extra-linguistic symbolic practices in the two cultures, such as what I call Americans' sportsmanization of politicians and politicianization of sportsmen and the Chinese traditional belief and practice in offering food to God and the dead.

Understanding the dominant metaphors of a language may enable us to gain a better appreciation of the people who speak the language and their culture. For those involved in anthropology, intercultural communication, or the study of a second or foreign language, it is thus very important and beneficial to study dominant metaphors of the languages of their interest. It is my hope this book may be of help to individuals working in these fields, especially in Sino-American studies or American English or Chinese as

Being one individual's endeavor, this book is, of course, limited in scope and depth. Furthermore, no single book can adequately cover the dominant metaphors in even one language, not to mention two. It is my sincere hope, though, that this book will generate more interest in American and Chinese metaphors and in metaphor use in general. What I have done here amounts to nothing more than, to use a Chinese proverb, *casting out some bricks in order to elicit jades* (from others). I have no doubt that some valuable jades will soon appear, and I look forward to reading them!

Glossary of Dominant Metaphorical Idioms

(Arranged in order by language and metaphor category)

American English

Business Metaphors

Asset or *credit*: the property, money, etc. that a person or organization has; Figurative meaning (FM hereafter): a valuable person, trait, etc.

Bail someone/something out: to pay the court-set amount of money to have an accused person released from and stay out of jail until the trial; FM: to rescue someone or something that is failing or in trouble because of some mistake.

Bank on: to bank is to invest money in a bank in the expectation of retrieving it for future use; FM: to depend on.

Bargain for something: to negotiate a price for something; FM: to ask for or expect something, often used in the negative form, e.g. "We didn't bargain for trouble; we just wanted to have some fun."

Bargaining chips: money or valuables used in commercial negotiations; FM: a leverage in negotiation in anything.

Be (back) in business: FM: be in operation again.

Cash in (on something): make money on something; FM: to take advantage of something.

(The) bottom line is . . .: the last line on a balance sheet; FM: the most important thing/point, or to go directly to the point.

Budget time: FM: to plan and use time wisely.

Business: commercial or monetary dealings; FM: 1) profession (e.g. "What business are you in?") 2) things, concerns, etc. (e.g. "I've some personal business" "It's none of your business.").

Buy an argument, idea, etc.: FM: to accept as valid or agree with an argument, etc.

Buy a good review, time, etc.: FM: to obtain or gain a good review, time, etc.

Buy into an argument, idea, etc.: FM: to believe in an argument, etc.

Byproduct: something created in the process of producing the principal product; FM: a secondary and often unintended or unexpected result of an action.

Cheap shot or *fire a cheap shot*: FM: (to launch) an unfair attack on someone.

Get more than one bargained for: FM: to suffer unexpected consequences that resulted from one's action.

Give credit to someone for something: FM: to attribute success, etc. to someone.

Feel like a million dollars: to feel being worth a million dollars; FM: to feel very good.

Give (or *put in*) *one's two cents' worth* (also *a penny's worth*): FM: to give or share one's thought or opinion.

Have someone or something as an asset: FM: to have someone as a valuable member, etc.

Have someone or something as a liability: FM: to have someone as a negative burden.

Live up to the billing: to prove that something/someone is worth the charged price; FM: to demonstrate something/someone is as valuable/true as it was originally claimed to be.

Market something: to try to persuade people to purchase something; FM: to persuade other people to accept something such as an idea, agenda, etc., or to hire a person.

Million-dollar question: FM: a very important question.

On the money: FM: completely correct on an issue.

On the other side of the coin: FM: from the other side's point of view.

Pay off: to completely pay back a loan; FM: to compensate in money or other means as a benefit for an earlier action on one's behalf or for an action or effort to produce benefits. The opposite is *"Doesn't pay off."*

Pay-off: a compensation for or benefit from an earlier action.

Pay a price: FM: to suffer consequences for an action.

Put in one's two cents worth: FM: to give one's humble opinion.

Put one's money where one's mouth is: FM: to be willing to support or prove one's claims.

Put stock in someone or something: to invest in something; FM: to place trust or belief in someone or something.

Retail (*politics* or *something*): small-scale practice/engagement.
Sell an agenda, etc: FM: to persuade others to accept and support an agenda, etc.
Short changed: not being given all the expected change; FM: being cheated or unfairly treated.
To yield dividends: FM: to produce benefits or positive effects.
Wholesale (*politics, killing , etc.*): FM: large scale practice/engagement.

Driving-Related Metaphors

Back-seat driver: a passenger in the backseat who gives orders to the driver; FM: one who is not in charge but likes to give orders.
Be in/take the backseat: to be a passenger on the backseat; FM: to be a follower or play a passive role.
Be in/take the driver's seat: to drive the car; FM: to play a leader role in something.
Be in the high gear: to be driving in a high gear; FM: for an activity/ event to reach a intense state.
Be the engine of something: FM: to be the driving force or leader of something.
Crank up or *be cranked up*: to turn the crank of car's engine to start it; FM: to begin and be undergoing or to become prepared for something with great enthusiasm.
Gain a lot of mileage (*out of something*): to drive a long distance with excellent fuel economy; FM: to maximize the return of one's effort by making a right move or doing something effectively or smartly.
Give the green light to somebody or something: FM: to give the go ahead signal for doing something.
Go up a gear: FM: to raise the intensity to a new level in an activity.
Grease the wheels: to lubricate the wheels with grease; FM: to make things operate effectively and smoothly.
Live in the fast lane: FM: to live a busy or reckless hedonistic life.
Make a u-turn: to make a 180 degree change of direction going opposite to the original direction.
Put a brake on: FM: to stop something.
Running with all cylinders: with every cylinder of an engine operating; FM: a team being fully functional, i.e. every member of the team is working to help accomplish a task.
Shift/switch gears: to change from one gear to another during driving;

FM: to switch a to a new topic or new item in an activity such as a meeting.
Spinning the wheels: the wheels running but not moving as sometimes in the case of driving on ice; FM: wasting efforts.
Step on it: to step on the accelerator: FM: to speed up or work harder on something.
With three cylinders running: without all the cylinders of an engine operating; FM: a team not being fully functional, i.e. not every member of a team is working to help the team.

Sports metaphors
(Limited by space, only metaphors from baseball, boxing, and American football are included)

Baseball

Ballpark figures: there are two versions of the origin of the idiom: one is that in old days, for lack of accurate counting methods, the report of the number of attendants at a baseball game was basically estimation; the other version, according to Palmatier and Ray's (1993, p. 8) *Dictionary of sports idioms*, is that historically the dimensions of baseball parks often vary from one to another, i.e. they are estimated to be closely the same; FM meaning: an approximate estimate of a number of something.
The bases are loaded: each base is occupied by a runner so the offensive team is very close to scoring; FM: a task is about to be accomplished.
Be out in left field: to take one of the three outfield defensive positions, and, according to Palmatier and Ray (1993, p. 126), left field "is part of the outfield that where the sun and the wind play tricks with the ball, and the walls and fans contribute to the 'terror'"; FM: to be without reason or erroneous.
Be out of bounds: the batted ball flies outside the boundaries of the playing field (now also used in other sports like basketball and football); FM: to behave inappropriately.
Bench a player: to move a player off the field, i.e. out of action; FM: to remove someone from duty.
Bench-player: a player that does not participate in action; FM: any team member who does not really participate in action.

Glossary of Dominant Metaphorical Idioms

Cover all the bases: to have defensive players guard every base against the advance of runners from the offensive team; FM: to take all the necessary actions so that a task can proceed successfully or one is protected.

Get to first base: to hit a single off the pitcher and advance to first base; FM: to make an initial advance or progress with someone or something.

Give or take a rain check: the old practice of allowing spectators a free second visit to a game that has been rained out and re-scheduled; FM: to give or accept promise of a service or agreement whereby the promise will be arranged, accommodated, and accepted in the future.

Have/carry a lot of clout: to be able to hit a baseball a long distance FM: to have a lot of power or influence.

Have a lot on the ball (also *have something on the ball*): to be able to pitch a baseball with great speed; FM: to have great talent in something.

Have an off day: to play "as if no game were scheduled, therefore no statistics"; FM: to give a substandard performance, not performing as well as one usually does (Palmatier and Ray, 1993, p. 74).

Hit a grand slam: to hit a home run while runners were on all the bases, therefore scoring four runs (the best type of home run); FM: to attain a great success or an ultimate achievement.

Hit a home run or hit a homer: to round all the bases and score at least a run with only one swing of the bat; FM: to achieve a great success.

Off base: to be off base and be tagged out; FM: to be erroneous, miss the point or behave inappropriately.

Play ball: when the umpire shouts, "play ball," the game begins; FM: to start working, to cooperate.

Play hard ball: to play the over-handed, fast pitch baseball as opposed to the underhanded, slow pitch softball; FM: to engage in a highly intense competitive endeavor or face a challenge.

Off the bat or *right of the bat*: the fast flying ball quickly off the bat when it hits the bat; FM: quickly and abruptly.

Step up to the plate: the hitter steps to the plate to be ready to play and to try to score; FM: to become prepared and ready to try one's utmost to accomplish something.

Strike out: to fail to hit the ball while batting, constituting one of the three units necessary to end that half of the inning; FM: to fail in an effort or enterprise.

Switch-hitter: a hitter that can bat right-handed as well as left-handed; FM: someone equally skilled at the one endeavor as another.

Throw a curve ball: to throw a ball that appears to stay in the strike zone but will curve out before it reaches the catcher; FM: to deceive or to surprise.

Touch base with: in order to hit a run, a hitter has to touch each of the three bases; FM: to communicate or consult with someone.

To touch all the bases: to touch all three of the bases plus the plate in order to score; FM: to take all the necessary precautions and get all the necessary approvals.

Boxing

Drop your guard: "to lower your hands, especially the 'lead' hand, during a fight, thereby leaving your head unprotected from the blows by your opponent"; FM: "to leave yourself unprotected from attack" (Palmatier and Ray, 1993, p. 43).

Hit below the belt: since it is against boxing rules to hit the opponent below the belt, to hit below the belt is considered an unfair play; FM: to do things unfairly or against the rules. Sometimes the expression "it's under the belt" is also used to refer to an unfair practice.

Heavyweight: a boxer in the heavyweight class; FM: a person of influence or statue in a field.

Knock someone out or *knock someone cold*: to hit the opponent so forcefully that the latter loses consciousness for at least the count of ten; FM: to give someone an stunning impression or to defeat someone instantly. Also the noun form *knockout* and its adjectival use in *a knockout blow*.

Knock yourself out: FM: cause your own defeat or failure.

On the ropes: pinned against or hanging on the ropes of the ring; FM: in serious trouble, defenseless.

Let someone off when you had him on the ropes: FM: to let someone get away or escape from a defeat when you had rendered the person defenseless and cornered.

One-two punch: an attack that involves two punches; FM: an attack on two fronts.

Pulling punches: withholding punches; FM: withholding criticism.

Saved by the bell: not pronounced defeated simply because the time of the fight has run out, i.e. the ringing of the bell; FM: rescued from a

disastrous situation at the last minute.
Throw in the towel: to throw a towel into the ring to signal that the boxer is giving up the fight; FM: to admit abandoning one's effort or admit defeat.

Football (American)

Call an audible: to change the offensive plan; FM: to change one's mind.
Call the play or make the play: to decide which play to use, a responsibility usually taken by the coach or the quarterback; FM: to designate decision-making responsibility.
Carry the ball: take leadership/responsibility: the offensive player, likely either the quarterback, running back, or receiver, carries the ball trying to gain yardage in order to score; FM: to take main responsibility or work load.
Drop the ball: the quarterback or any player who held the ball drops it; FM: to fail to fulfill one's responsibility.
Get in a huddle: players meet, prior to the play, in very close proximity to each other for the purpose of deciding and/or communicating the chosen play to the offensive and defensive unit on the field; FM: to have an informal meeting in order to communicate strategy.
Level the playing field (also *playing on a level field*): to make the playing field level so as to be fair to both teams; FM: to make sure of a fair condition for any competition, be it business or politics.
Monday morning quarterbacking: to comment on how a football should have been played; FM: offering after-the fact suggestions/advice.
On the sideline: being on the sideline waiting to participate in a game; FM: waiting and looking for opportunities to participate.
Play offensive/defensive: in a game at a given point, one side is playing offensive and the other is playing defense; FM: to use various strategies to launch an offense/attack when playing offense and to practice various strategies to stage a defense when playing defensive.
Play on other people's turf: FM: to invade and conduct business in other people's field.
Punt the ball: to kick the ball to the other team's side after failing to gain ten yards after three trials (a team can have up to four trials yet if it fails in the fourth attempt, the other team will have the advantage of starting offense where you failed, often meaning a

much better offensive position); FM: to give up an opportunity to try and fight or to yield one's responsibility.
Quarterback (verb): FM: to direct and lead an offense or activity.
Run with the ball(it): to carry and move forward with the ball; FM: to take the lead and try to accomplish the task at hand.
Score a touchdown: to carry the ball into the opponent's end zone; FM: to win a major victory or to achieve a significant accomplishment in a cause/task.
Take the ball and run with it: FM: to take leadership in carrying out a Task.

Chinese

Eating and Food Metaphors

Those that start with or contain the word chi ["eat"]

Chi baizan: to eat a defeat; FM: to suffer a defeat.
Chi bimengen: to eat a closed-door soup; FM: to find the door closed, i.e. be denied entrance, when one tries to pay a visit to a person or place, meaning being not welcome.
Chi buliao dozhe zo: to not be able to finish the food that one has asked for or got oneself so the person has to carry it away in his/her lap; FM to get oneself into trouble by trying to be smart, something close to the English idiom "to get more than one bargained for." It is not as close to the English idiom "to bite more than one can chew" which means that one has taken on more than one can accomplish," not necessarily to get oneself into trouble.
Chi buxiao: not able to eat and digest anymore; FM: not able to stand/ bear something.
Chi cu: to eat vinegar; FM: to be jealous.
Chi dekai: to eat openly; FM: to be popular or to be able to have one's own way easily.
Chi dexiao: to be able to eat and digest; FM: to be able to stand exertion, fatigue, hardships, etc.
Chi dezhu moren: to be able to eat someone firmly; FM: to be able to handle someone.

Glossary of Dominant Metaphorical Idioms 129

Chi de yan bini chi de fan haiduo: the salt I have eaten is more than the rice you have eaten; FM: I am by far more experienced than you.
Chi diao diren: to eat up all the enemy: FM: to wipe out the enemy
Chi din (or *chi zhu*) *moren*: to eat someone for sure; FM: to have total control of someone or to be able to take full advantage of someone.
Chi dinxinwan: to eat a mind-easing pill; FM: to be reassured.
Chi guansi: to eat a lawsuit; FM: to face a lawsuit or to be sued.
Chi jin: to eat a surprise; FM: to be startled or surprised.
Chi jin: to eat tenseness; FM: (for a situation) to be serious or critical.
Chi jin: for a task to eat force; FM: for a task to require a tremendous force or to be challenging.
Chi jiuji: to eat welfare; FM: to live on welfare.
Chi ku: to eat bitterness; FM: to endure hardship.
Chi kui: to eat hidden losses; FM: to suffer undue or undeserving losses.
Chi kutou: to eat bitterness head; FM: to experience sufferings.
Chi laoben: to eat one's past accomplishments/glories; FM: to live on one's past accomplishments.
Chi le baozhidan: to have eaten a leopard's or panther's gall; FM: to be extremely but also unreasonably bold (a negative comment).
Chi li pawai: to eat the inside but scrape things out; FM: to live on one's own family or friends while secretly helping an outsider.
Chi neitao: to eat a practice, an attitude, etc.; FM: to accept a practice or attitude by another person directed toward the speaker. Often the expression is used in the negative form toward the interlocutor to show defiance, e.g. *wo buchi ni neitao* (I do not eat your practice, Etc.).
Chi (nuren de) doufu: to eat a woman's tofu; FM: to make a sexual advance towards a woman.
Chi ruan bu chi yin: to eat softness but not hardness; FM: to accept or be open to gentle persuasion but not coercion.
Chi tou (something): to eat something thoroughly; FM: to gain a full grasp of a theory, a book, etc.
Chi xianchenfan: to eat a ready meal; FM: to live off others' effort.
Chi zhai: to eat vegetables only; FM: to practice abstinence.
Chi xianfan: to eat lazy rice/meal; FM: to fool around without doing any work.
Chi xiang: to eat fragrance; FM: to be very popular or to be able to have one's way.
Chi yijian: to eat a chasm or eat a fall; FM: to make a mistake.

Chi zhewanfan: to eat this bowl of rice; FM: to make a living in this profession.
Da chi xiao: big[ger] eats small[er]; FM: the strong preys on the weak (as the law of the jungle); see also *ruorou qiangshi*.
kao x chi fan: to eat (rice) by something, i.e. by looks or talents; FM: to live by or make a living by something such as by looks or by kissing up to one's boss.
Kaoshan chi shan; kaoshui chi shui: to eat mountains if you live near mountains and to eat water if you live near water; FM: to make your living and survive by exploiting the resources of mountains if you live nearby mountains etc.
Yin chi mao liang: eat, in the year of yin, the grain of the year of mao (the year of yin comes before the year of mao); FM: spend or use up future resources

Other eating and food metaphors

Chao gu: to fry stocks; FM: to trade stocks
Chao jufan: to fry leftover rice; FM: to repeat saying or doing something old (to have nothing new to add)
Chao youyu: to fry squids; FM: to fire someone from a job.
Chaozhuo xinwen: to fry a news story; FM: to stir up a news story or turn something trivial into something sensational.
Diu fanwan: to lose one's rice bowl; FM: to lose one's job.
Fantong: a rice barrel; FM: a good-for-nothing person.
Hele henduo moshi deren: a person who has drunk a lot of ink; a very learned person.
Lao youshui: to scoop oil water [traditionally believed to be the best part of a dish]; FM: to take advantage of something or occasion often at the expense of others
Pianshi: to eat a one-sided diet; FM: to read only certain types of books, etc. or to nurture or entertain a one-sided view.
Rang zhushude yazi feile: to let a cooked duck fly away; FM: let go of a sure victory or fail to complete an almost finished task.
Ruorou qiangshi: the weak is the food of the strong; FM: the strong preys on the weak (the law of the jungle); see also *da chi xiao*.
Shenmi zhuchenle shufan: the raw rice has already been cooked; FM: it is too late to change anything in the situation.
Wan wei: play taste; FM: be interesting. Compare also *you qu wei* ("have fun taste" meaning "be interesting") and *yi wei* ("meaning

taste," meaning "indicate').
Wengzhong zibie: a turtle in the cooking pot; FM: someone that has no chance of escaping or a sure thing.
Yin chi mao lian: to eat in the year of *yin* (a number-like word standing for a year in the Chinese traditional year counting system with sixty years as a cycle) the food that belongs to the year of *mao*; FM: to overspend by spending future money or resources.
Yin chou or *yin hen*: to drink hatred; FM: nurture/harbor hatred.
Yin dan: to drink bullets; FM: to be killed by a bullet.
Yin zhen zi ke: to drink poison to quench thirst; to seek temporary relief or satisfaction regardless of the dire consequences the action will bring.
Yi shui siyuan: to think of its source when you drink water; FM: never forget the origin or the causes of your success.
Yin ye fei shi: to stop eating all together because of having choked once; FM: to discard the whole thing simply because part of it is bad or harmful, similar to the English expression "throwing out the baby with the bath water."
Yige heshang tiaoshui chi; liangge heshang tashui chi; sange heshang meishui chi: an only monk will obtain drinking water by carrying it himself; with two monks, they will obtain drinking water by carrying it together; with three monks, they will have not water to drink; FM: when there are many people involved in one project, people tend to rely on others to accomplish the task often resulting in the task being unable to be completed.
Ying zhe tong chi: Winner eats all; FM: Winner takes all.
Zha guole: the cooking pot is broken; FM: something has gone completely wrong and is beyond repair.

Family-Related Metaphors

Baijia zi: a family-ruining son; FM: a person that ruins an institution, nation, etc.
Chang jia: factory/plant family; FM: a factory or company.
Chuangjia bao: a treasure that has been passed on from generation to generation in a family; FM: any valuable thing or traditional practice that has come down from previous generation and is still valued.
Dangjia: to manage (the) family; FM: to be in charge.
Dao jia: to reach family/home; FM: to reach the highest level in

something. For instance, if someone's skills have perfected, then his skills can be said to have *dao jia*.

Du jia (baodao/xinwen): the sole family's report/news; FM: the only (news) agency to be reporting the news.

Fumu guang: father-mother-officials; FM: officials in your hometown, state, etc.

Gujia guaren: sole family, lone person; FM: a loner.

Gong Jia: public family; FM: the state (often used to refer to the opposite of "private"); Also *gong jai de*: public family's; FM: the state's or the public's.

Guojia: state-family; FM: state.

Jiachan: family property; FM: the property of any institution, nation, etc.

Jiachang: common family or trivial chores; FM: common daily activities or small talk as used in *la jiachang*.

Jiachang bianfan: daily family meals; FM: common occurrence or routine.

jiachang hua: common family talk; FM: small talk.

Jiachou: family scandal; FM: scandal in an institution/organization.

jiachou buke waiyang: Family scandals should not be made public; FM: don't publicize an institution's scandals or negative things.

Jiadang: (same as *jiachan*).

Jiadi: total family property and resources; FM: the total property and resources of any Institution.

Jia tianxia: family heaven and earth; FM: a family-controlled/operated institution or nation.

Jiatu sibi: an empty family house with merely four walls; FM: destitute.

Jiayu fuxiao: know to every family and household; FM: known to everyone.

Jiaye: family property; the property of any institution.

Jiazei: a thief within the family; FM: a thief or enemy within an institution/organization.

Jiazhang: family head, meaning parents, hence *jiazhang hei*: teacher parents conference.

Kanjia benling: skills for watching and protecting one's family; FM: one's best skill and performance.

Liang gu zhijian nan weifu: it is difficult to be a woman between a mother-in-law and sister-in-law; FM: it is difficult to exist and keep a balance between two powers.

Qinjian cijia: to frugally sustain a family; FM: frugally running any organization.

Qingjia dangchan: the whole family's properties and valuables are lost; FM: for any person or institution to lose all his/its properties and valuables.

Rushu jiazhen: counting one's family assets; FM: being very familiar with an issue, topic, etc.

So and so jia: so and so family; FM: so and so school of thought such as *yu jia* ("Confucian family" or Confucian school of thought) and *fa jia* ("Legalist family" or the Legalist school of thought).

So and so *zijia*: so and so family such as Dancers' family; FM: referring to a place/institution for a specific group of people to enjoy their hobby.

Tong bao: children born to the same parents; FM: one's fellow countrymen.

Yeye shichong sunzhi zhuoqide: Grandfathers grow out of grandchildren; FM: any successful person in a profession must start from scratch and experience a lot of suffering before he/she can become an established player in it. For example, in a news report ("Beijing vagrant singers: Striving for survival and chasing dreams" News.Sinanet, October 2, 1998) about how unknown singers strive for survival and success in Beijing, one such singer was quoted to say that he was suffering many hardships for not having regular performance sites or a fixed income but he was not complaining because *"to be a grandpa one must first be a grandson."*

Opera/acting metaphors

Chang bai lian: to sing in white face (in Beijing opera, characters painted with a white face are bad guys); FM: to play the bad guy. The expression is often used in conjunction with *chang honglian* (see below).

Chang (bao chi) di diao: To sing or keep a low tune; FM: to act cautiously by not drawing attention to oneself, i.e. to keep a low profile.

Chang dujiao xi: to put on a one-person show; FM: to implement or carry out something without any support from others, often used negatively.

Chang dutai xi: to sing the opposite part; FM: to take an opposite position against a person or to oppose someone on an issue. It is similar to *chang fan dia* (see below).

Chang fan diao: to sing the opposite tune; FM: to take an opposite position against a person or to oppose someone on an issue. It is similar to *change dui tai xi* (see above).

Chang hong lian: to sing in red face (in Beijing opera, characters painted with a red face are good guys); FM: to play the nice guy. The expression is often used in conjunction with *chang bai lian*, e.g. you'll sing in the red face and I'll sing in the white face.

Chang gao diao: sing a high tune; FM: to take a high moral ground.

Chang shuang huang: to put on a special two-person comedy where one person hides behind the other to provide mostly the voice performance while the other at the front provide most of the physical performance; FM: two people stage a scheme to cheat others.

(Chang) ya zhou xi: to present the last item in a performance; FM: to give the last but also the most important and often the best item or part of something.

Chang zhu jue: to sing the leading role; FM: to play the leading role in an activity/event.

Deng tai: to mount a stage; FM: to take an important position or to be in power.

Feng chang zuo xi: to act a performance according to the occasion; FM: to do or say something simply to please people, i.e. not seriously.

Fu chang fu sui: when a husband sings, the wife follows; FM: in a family, the wife plays Only a supporting role for her husband—doing and saying whatever her husband does or says.

Jin luo mi gu: to beat gongs and drums fast and loud (in Beijing opera, it signals the imminent raising of the curtain, i.e. the beginning of an act; FM: to engage in an intense publicity campaign to signal the imminent undertaking of an important cause/action/policy (often used negatively).

Mei xi chang le: no more opera to sing; FM: there is no more hope for or it is the end of something. The opposite expression is *you xi chang* (see below).

Pao long tao: To run through the stage or to make a very short appearance on the stage as secondary actors do in playing unimportant characters or masses; FM: to play an insignificant role or to do something unimportant and routine *Self-directed and self-acted out drama*: FM: to design and does something as a scheme for a mischievous or wicked purpose.

Shang tai or *Xia tai*: to get on or get off the stage; FM: *shang tai* means to take (0ver) and function in an important position and *xiatai* means to step down from an important position in an institution or government.

Tiao liang xiaochou: A clown jumping on a beam; FM: (very derogatorily) a person who is trying to make a show but only ends up showing his/her stupidity or ignorance.

You xi chang: there is opera; FM: there is still a lot to be played out or there is still a lot to be decided.

References

A major budget victory. (1995, January 29). *The Sunday Oklahoman*, p. A10.
Albright: No apologies. (1999, March 2). *BBC News* [Online]. Retrieved from: www.news.bbc.co.uk/hi.
Aristotle. (1946). *Rhetoric*. (W. R Roberts, Trans.). In W. D. Ross (Ed.) *The works of Aristotle translated into English* (Vol. 11). Oxford: Oxford UP
Ba Dun. (May 2, 2002). Hu Jintao di dia bi gao dia hao [Low tune is better than high tune for Hu Jintao]. *Duo Wei Xinwen She* [*Chinese News Net*] [Online]. Retrieved from: www.chinesenewsnet.com.
Barnathan, J. (1995, March 20). Has Singapore got what it takes to be a financial power house. *Business Week*, pp. 54-56.
Bloomfield, Frena. (1983). *The book of Chinese beliefs: A Compendium of philosophy, customs, and healing traditions*. New York: Allentine books.
Cao Changqing. (2001, December 3). Pujin he Jiang Zeming: Bubi bu zhidao [Ptin and Jiang Zemin: Not knowing without comparing]. [Online] Retrieved from: www.Chinesenewsnet.com.
Cao Zhi-yuan. (1995, July 30). Yi naixin chu qi jinbu yi aixin chu qi xinsheng: zhongguo wenti mouzhou jiduan [Promote progress with patience and cultivate new life with love: No extremism allowed for the China problem]. *Shijie Zoukan*, p. S3.
Carroll, J. B. (1963). Linguistic relativity, contrastive linguistics, and langauge learning. *International Review of Applied Linguistics in Language Teaching 1*, 1-20.
Casteel, C. (1996, November 6). Sooners in Congress hope for balanced budget law. *The Daily Oklahoman*, p. A8.
Chang Fang-ming. (2001, August 3). Xiaoquan shouxiang rang tianzhong nu yaixiang linjao shita dangjai zuozhu [Prime Minister Joizumi taught the Foreign Affairs Minister Tanaka that "it is he who manages the family and is the master]. *Duo Wei Xinwen She*

[*Chinese News Net*] [Online]. Retrieved from: www.Chinesenewsnet.com.

Chen Hongyi. (2000, November1). Wu Mingxi shuo Taiwan wenti shi jiawushi yairen burong ganyu [Wu Mingxi said Taiwan is a family problem and no outsiders should be allowed to interfere]. *Zhongguo Ribao* [Online]. Retrieved from: www.usnews.sina.com/zhongguo.

Chen Shui-bian cheng liangan shi yijiaren [Chen Shui-bian calls the two sides across the Strait one family]. *Fenghuang Xinwen* [Online]. Retrieved from: www.cnnews.sina.com/phoenixtv.

Chen Shui-bian: Haixia liangan shi yijia [Chen Shui-bian: The two sides across the Strait are one family]. (2000, May 17). *Fenghuang Xinwen* [Online]. Retrieved from: www.cnnews.sina.com/phoenixtv.

Chen, Ying-Ying. (2000, June 6). Lü Hsiu-lien y jiating baoli shouhai she biyu Taiwan [Lü Hsiu-lien compares Taiwan to a victim of family violence] [Online]. Retrieved from: www.twnews.sina.com/ckp/twpolitics.

Chi an: Jincha chi an xilie [Eat cases: A series about police eating cases]. (1999, April 22). *Zhongguo Shibao* [Online]. Retrieved from: www.sina.com/news/chinatimes.

Chunjie wanhui zhe dao cai zhende shou le ma [Has the New Year's Even Show really gone bad]? (Feb. 12, 2002). *Duo Wei Xinwen She* [*Chinese News Net*] [Online]. Retrieved from: www.chinesenewsnet.com.

Chunjie lianhuan wanhui ha zhong qu chong, fenshi taiping [The New Year's Eve Show a claptrap attempting to paint a rosy picture]. (Feb. 14, 2002). *Do Wei Xinwen She* [*Chinese News Net*] [Online]. Retrieved from: www.chinesenewsnet.com

Cigler, Allen, J. and Loomis, Burdett A. (Eds.). (1983). *Interest group politics*. Washington, D.C.: Congressional Quarterly Press.

Coakley, J. (1994). *Sports in Society: Issues and Controversies* (5th ed.). St. Louis: Mosby.

Concluding the trial. (1999, February 4). *Nightline*. New York: ABC.

Constructive polarization. (1996, November 12). *The Daily Oklahoman*, p. A4.

Deng, Xiaoping. (1993). *Deng Xiaoping Wenxuan* [*Anthology of Deng Xiaoping Works*], Vol. 3. Beijing: Renmin Chubanshe.

Deng, Xiaoping. (1983). *Deng Xiaoping Wenxuan* [*Anthology of Deng Xiaoping Works*]. Vol. 2. Beijing: Renmin Chubanshe.

Ditch the `Final Four' Banner. (1999, February 28, 1999). *The Daily Oklahoman,* p. B3.

Eitzen, D. S. and G. H. Sage. 1993 *Sociology of North American sport* (5th ed.). Madison, Wisconsin: WBC Brown and Benchmark.

Elegant, R. S. (1959). *The dragon's seed: Peking and the overseas Chinese.* New York: St. Martin's Press.

Ellingwood, S. (1997, March 10). Domestic partners: China's codependents in the U.S. *The New Republic, 216*(10), 12-13.

Emanatian, M. (1999). Congruence by degree: On the relationship between metaphors & cultural models. In R. Gibbs and G. J. Steen (Eds.), *Metaphor in cognitivelinguistics* (pp. 205-218). Amsterdam: John Benjamins.

Fan Fu. (1996, March, 24). Cong shunkoliu kan zhongguo dalu [A look at Mainland China via doggerels]. *Shijie Zhoukan,* p. S7.

Fantini, A. (1995). Language, culture and worldview: Exploring the nexus. *International Journal of Intercultural Relations 19, 143-153.*

Fauconnier, G. (1994). *Mental spaces.* Cambridge: Cambridge University Press.

Fauconnier, G. (1997). *Mappings and thought and language.* Cambridge: Cambridge University Press.

Feng Tianyu and Zhou Jiming. (1989). *Zhongguo wenhua de mimi* [*The secrets of Chinese culture*]. Hong Kong: Nanyue Chubanshe.

Figler, S. K. and Whitaker, G. (1991). *Sports and play in American life* (2nd ed.). Dubuque, IA: WMC Brown.

Fiumara, G. C. (1995). *The metaphoric process: Connections between language and life.* New York: Routledge.

Flashpoint. (1998, November 22). Oklahoma City, OK: KFOR TV.

Friedman, E. (1995). *National identity and democratic prospects in socialist China.* Armonk, New York: M. E. Sharpe, Inc.

Fox Sunday News (1998, October 4). New York: The Fox News Network.

Gibbs, R. (1994). *The poetic of mind: Figurative thought, language, and understanding.* New York: Cambridge University Press.

Gibbs, R. (1996). Why many concepts are metaphorical. *Cognition, 61,* 309-319.

Gibbs, R. (1999). Taking metaphor out of our heads and putting it into the cultural world. In R. Gibbs and G. J. Steen (Eds.), *Metaphor in cognitive linguistics* (pp. 145-166). Amsterdam: John Benjamins.

Gibbs, R. and Steen, G. J. (Eds.). (1999). *Metaphor in cognitive*

linguistics. Amsterdam: John Benjamins.
Goatly, A. (1997). *The language of metaphors*. New York: Routledge.
Goodman, N. (1981) "Metaphor as moonlighting." In S. Sacks (Ed.), *On metaphor*. (pp. 175-180). Chicago: Chicago UP.
Gorman, J. and Calhoun, K. (1994). *The Name of the game: The business of sports*. New York: John Wiley & Sons.
Han Ying Cidia [*A Chinese–English Dictionary*]. (1980). Beijing: Sangwu chubanshe.
Hardaway, Francine. (1976). Foul play: Sports metaphor as public double speak. *College English, 38*, 78-82.
Hartman, D. (1998, February, 25). Academic bowl state title goes to Edmond team. *The Daily Oklahoman*, A 9.
Helyar, J. (1994). *Lords of the realm: The real history of American's game*. New York: Villard Books.
Hill, J. and Mannheim, B. (1992). Language and worldview. *Annual Review of Anthropology 21,* 381-406.
Hirsch, E. D., Kett, J. F., and Trefil, J. (1993). *The Dictionary of cultural literacy: What Every American Needs to Know*. 2nd Ed. Boston: Houghton Mifflin.
Huang, Annie. (2000, July 22). China TV program gets Taiwanese host [Online]. Retrieved from: www.dailynews.yahoo.com/h/ap.
Hymes, D. (1972). Models of the interaction of language and social life." In J. Gumperze and D. Hymes (Eds.), *Directions in sociolinguistics: The Ethnography of communication*. (pp. -72). New York: Holt, Rinehart & Winston.
In Jiang's words: "I hope the Western world can understand China better." (2001, August 10). *New York Times*, p. A8.
Is sports jargon pure jibberish? Just plain English please! (Nov. 5, 1995). *The SundayOklahoman*, p. C8.
Iso-Ahola, S. E. and Hatfield, B. 1986 *Psychology of sports: A social psychological approach*. Dubuque, Iowa: WM.C. Publishers.
Jia [family]. (1995). *Ci Yuan* [*Etymology of words*]. Revised and combined Ed. (p. 453). Beijing: Shangwu Chubanshe.
Jiang, Zemin. (1997). Wei cujin zhuguo tongyi daye de wancheng er jisxu fendou, January 30, 1995 [Continue to strive and push for the accomplishment of the grand task of unifying the motherland, January 30, 1995]. In Zhonggong Zhongyang Wenxian Yanjiushi (Ed.), *"Yiguo lainzhi" zhongyao wenxian xuanbian* [*Selectedimportant documents on "One country, two systems" policy*] (pp. 253-259), Beijing: Zhongyang Wenxian Chubanshe.

Jiang, Zemin. (2000, September 10). Taiwan shi zhong mei guanxi zui zhongyao de wenti [Taiwan is the most important issue in Sino America relationship]. *Guangzhou Ribao* (Online). Retrieved from: www.cnnews.sina.com/kwongzhou/china.

Jiang Zemin fang chaoxian: zou qinqi [Jiang Zemin's trip to North Korea: A visit to a relative]. (2001, September 3) [Online]. Retrieved from: www.chinesenewsnet.com.

Jiang, Zhaolun. (2001, April 4). Dailu daoyan Jiang Wen: *Wuo hu changlung* shi ershinian qian de dongxi [Mainland Director Jiang Wen: Crouching Tiger and Hidden Dragon, a thing of twenty years ago], *Dongseng Xinwen Bao* (Online). Retrieved from: www.dailynews.sina.com/newscenter/focusreport.

Kövecses, Z. (1999). Metaphor: Does it constitute or reflect cultural models? In R. Gibbs and G. J. Steen (Eds.). *Metaphor in cognitive linguistics* (pp. 167-188). Amsterdam: John Benjamins.

Lakoff, G. (1987). *Women, fire, and dangerous things.* Chicago: Chicago University Press.

Lakoff, G. (1990). The invariance hypothesis: Is abstract reason based on image-schemas?" *Cogntive Linguistics, 1*, 39-74.

Lakoff, G. and Johnson, M. (1980) *Metaphors we Live By.* Chicago: Chicago UP.

Lakoff, G. and Turner, M. (1989). *More than cool reason: A field guide to poetic metaphor.* Chicago: Chicago University Press.

Latourette, Kenneth Scott. (1964). *The Chinese, their history, and culture.* 4th Ed. New York: The Macmillan Company.

Lee Kuan Yew: Liangan butong budu jumian jiang dapo [Lee Kuan Yew: The no-unification-and-no-independence status will be changed]. (2000, September 23). *Qiaobao* [Online]. Retrieved from: www.usnews.sina.com/chinapress.

Lee Kuan Yew Jieshou zhuanfang [Lee Kuan Yew took an exclusive interview] (2001, January 23). *Mingri Bao* [Online]. Retrieved from: www.dailynews.sina.com/newscenter /foucs.

Lee Teng-hui huiying jiang badian zai guotonghui shang jianghua quanwen [Lee Teng- Hui's speech at the National Unification Commision in response to Jiang's Eight-point Statement]. (1995, April 9). *Shijie Ribao*, p. A2.

Lee Teng-hui shuo gaige yi Chiang Ching-Kuo weishi [Lee Teng-hui says he will follow Chiang Ching-Kuo in reform]. (1995, March 25). *Shijie Ribao*, p. A1.

Lee Teng-hui zhi tai shi fuqin dalu shi erzi [Lee Teng-hui calls Taiwan the father and Mainland China the son]. (1999, December 22). *Xincheng Diantai* [Online]. Retrieved from: www.twnews.sina.com/metro/hongkong.

Li Ge. (2000, May 14). Ye yang dianhua caifang Lü Hsiu-lien [Interviewing Lü Hsiu-lien via phone across the Pacific]. *SingtaoRibao* [Online]. Retrieved from: www.dailynews.sina.com/aemrica/singtao.

Liangan xiongdi guanxi, zhuquan juebu rangbu [The two sides across the Strait are brothers yet no concession on sovereignty]. (1995, April 6). *Shijie Ribao*, p. A1.

Lin Chuangcheng. (1996, May 27). Kezheng chi chunu [Tyrannical government eats virgins]. *Shijie Ribao*, p. B10.

Liu, D. (2000). "Hitting singles" and "Scoring runs": Sports metaphor in American English and American life as sports. *Alpha Vision: An Interdisciplinary Journal of Higher Education, 1*, 10-16.

Liu, D. (1999). The pride of *zuguo*: China's perennial appeal to the overseas Chinese and an emergent civic dicourse in a glabal community. In R. Kluver and J. Powers (Eds). Civic discourse, civial society, and Chinese communities (pp. 209-220). Stamford, CT : Ablex.

Liu, D. and Farha, B. (1996). "Three strikes and you're out": A study of the use of football and baseball jargon in present-day American English. *English Today: An international review of the English Language, 12*.1, 36-40.

Liu, Zhaifu. and Lin, Gang. (1988). *Chuangtong yu zhongguo ren* [*Tradition and the Chinese*]. Taipei, Taiwan: Renjian chubanshe.

Lowe, S. R. (1995). *The kid on the sandlot: Congress and professionalsprots 1910-1992*. Bowling Green, OH: Bowling Green State University Popular Press.

Luyou tuan liuxing jia fuqi jia muzi [Fake couples and fake mother-son couples common in tourist groups]. *Zhongguo Qinian Bao* report carried in *Guangzhou Ribao*, [Online]. Retrieved from: www.cnnews.sina.com/Guangzhou/china.

Lu, Xun. (1981). A madman's diary. In *The complete stories of Lu Xun* (X. Yang and G. Yang, Trans.), (pp. 1-12). Bloomington: Indiana University.

Ma Dao-rong. (2000, April 21). Yao dong zuo ke daoli [It is necessary to understand the rules for guest behavior] [Online]. Retrieved from: www.dailynews.sina.com/newscenter.

Maikovich, A. J. (Ed.). (1984) *Sports quotations: Maxims, quips and pronouncements for writers and fans.* Jefferson, NC: McFarland and Company.

McGuigan, P. B. (1995, January 29). Lame duck & right wingers. *The Sunday Oklahoman,* p. A10.

Meet the Press. (1998, November 8). New York: NBC.

Meng, X. (1995). Zhong mei tai guanxi de bianhua: Taiwan fuchude daijia [The change of relationships between China, Taiwan, and America: The price Taiwan paid]. *Shijie Ribao,* July 19. p. A2.

Moise, E. (1994). *The present and the past: Modern China: A history* (2nd ed). New York: Longman.

Muhlhausler, Peter. (1995). Metaphors others live by. *Language and Communication 15,* 281-288.

Nance, Roscoe. (1998, June 1). Pacers don't find solace in taking bulls to the limit. *USA Today,* p. C3.

Naylor, B. (1998, November 18). *Morning Edition.* Washington D. C.: NPR.

The News Hour with Jim Lehrer. (1997, May 13). Washington D.C.: Public Broadcasting Service.

Nixon, H. L. II. (1984). *Sport and the American Dream.* New York: Leisure Press.

Nothing to be sorry for. (1996, September 2). *Sports Illustrated,85*(10), 18.

Ong, A. & Nonini, D. M. (Eds.). (1997). *Ungrounded empire: The cultural politics of modern Chinese tansnationalism.* New York: Routledge.

Palmatier, R. and Ray, H. (1993). *Dictionary of sports idioms.* Lincolnwood, IL: NTC.

Plato. (1961). *The collected dialogues of Plato.* Eds. Edith Hamilton and Huntington Cairns. New York: Bollingen Foundation/Pantheon Books.

Plato. (1992). *Repupblic.* Trans. G.M.A. Grube, Revised C.E.C. Reeve. Indianapolis: Hackett Publishing Company.

Qian, Qicheng (2001, January 23). Zai jilian Jiang Zemin duitai zhongyao jianghua liu zhounian huishangdi jianghua [Speech at the gathering marking the sixth anniversary of Jiang Zemin's important statement about Taiwan]. *China NewsService* [Online]. Retrieved from: www.cnnews.sina.com/chinanews/china.

Qian Qichen: Liangan doushi zhongguo bu chunzai shuichishude wenti [Qian Qichen:Both sides are China so no such problem of who eating up who]." (2000, July 19). *Guoji Ribao* [Online]. Retrieved

from: www.usnews.sina.com/cntoday/headline.
Rader, D. (August 19, 2001). Nothing could stop me but me. *Parade* (a *Sunday Oklahoma* magazine), pp. 4-5.
Roberts, R. and Olson, J. (1989). *Winning is the only thing: Sports in America since 1945*. Baltimore: Johns Hopkins University Press.
Ross, B. Jr. (1997, June 23). For some, only perfection will do. *The Daily Oklahoman/Oklahoma City Times*, II, pp. 1, 3.
Rukeyser, L. (1995, June 30). *Wall Street week with Louis Rukeyser*. Owings Mills, MD: Maryland Public Television.
Rukeyser, L. (1999, January 29). *Wall Street week with Louis Rukeyser*. Owings Mills, MD: Maryland Public Television.
Russert, T. (1998, November 3). *Meet the Press*. New York: NBC.
Seinfeld. (1994, November 10).
Seinfeld. Rock Entertainment. Beverly Hills and NBC.
Shengwei shuji pai an che chihe [Provincial Party Secretary angrily condemns eating/drinking parties]. (2001, January 18). *Yangcheng Wanbao* [Oneline]. Retrieved from: www.cnnews.sina.com/yceve/china.
Shiff, R. (1981). Art and Life: A Metaphoric Relationship. in S. Sacks (Ed.), *On Metaphor*, (pp. 105-120). Chicago: Chicago UP.
Shunde: ganjin buzhun chi dangshi ren [Police officers: Not allowed to eat individuals involved in the case]. (2000, June 13). *GuangzhouRibao* [Online]. Retrieved from: www.cnnews.sina.com/Guangzhou/canton.
Shixian zhongguo tongyi shi zhe yidairen lish zeren [Accomplishing unification of China is this generation's historical task]. (2000, July 3). *Qiaobao* [Online]. Retrieved from: www.usnews.sina.com/chinapress/usa.
Soft money game. (1998, November, 2). *Nightline*. Chris Bury. New York: ABC.
Sowell, Thomas. (1999, October 26). School choice wars heating up. *The Daily Oklahoman*, p. A. 5)
Starr, Paul. (1997, March/April). Democracy v. dollar. *The American Prospect, 8*, 6-9.
Still standing. (1998, October 5) *Time 152*. p. 21.
The President and the election. (1998, October 28). *Nightline*. New York: ABC.
The White House defense. (1999, January 20). *Nightline*. New York: ABC.
Today Show (1995, June 21). New York: NBC.

Totenburg, N. (1998, November 5). *Morning Edition*. Washington D.C.: NPR.
Vietnamese Flag dropped off brochure. (2001, August 12). *Sunday Oklahoman*, p. A22
Vogler, C. C. and S. E. Schwartz. (1993). *The Sociology of sport: An introduction*. Englewood Cliffs, New Jersey: Prentice Hall.
Wahlgren, Eric. (1999, July 18). Week of reckoning for earnings [Online]. Retrieved from: www.dailynews.yahoo.com/headline/reuters.
Wang, G. (Ed.). *China and the overseas Chinese*. Singapore: Times Academic Press.
Wang, Jun. (2001, December 21). Zuo cai yu zi guo [Cooking and ruling a country] [Online]. Retrieved from: www.chinesenewsnet.com.
Wang Li-juan. (1998, December 29). Shao Yu-Ming: Beijing buying dui tai bihun [Shao Yuming: Beijing should not pressure Taiwan into marriage]. *Shijie Ribao*, p. A2.
Wang Lixiong. (1998, December 6). Zhongguo wenhua jiegoude jieti he jieshu [The deconstruction and the end of the structure of Chinese culture]. *Shijie zhoukan*, pp. 26-27.
Wang Luowang. (1996, February 18). Nanhan shi dalude yimian "jingzi" [South Korea is a "mirror" of the Mainland China]. *ShijieZoukan*, p. S3.
Wang Yun. (August, 24). "Renwu chexie" qiang dujia: zongminhua fengyun zhaiqi ["Exclusive personal interviews": Connie Chung suddenly re-rises] [Online]. Retrieved from: www.content.sina.com/news.
Wayne, Stephen. J. (2001). *Is this any way to run a democratic election?* Boston: Houghton Mifflin Company.
Wehrfritz, George. (1995, May 22). A New Emperor Ascendant? *News Week*, p. 35.
Weiss, A. E. (1993). *Money Games: The Business of Sports*. Boston: Houghton Mifflin.
White House Defends Talks. (1995). An Associated Press report carried in *The Daily Oklahoman*, May 12, pp. A1-2.
Whorf, B. L. (1956). *Language, Thought, and Reality: Selected Writings*. Cambridge, Mass: MIT Press.
Wierzbicka, A. (1991). *Cross-cultural pragmatics: The semantics of human interaction*. New York: Mouton de Gruyter.
Wierzbicka, A. (1992). *Semantics, culture, and cognition: Universal*

human concepts in culture-specific configuration. New York: Oxford University Press.

Wiessler, David. (1998, November 4). Democrats back in business after U.S. elections [Online]. Retrieved from: www.dailynews.yahoo.com/headline.

Williams, Walter. (1997, May 9). "Improve education: Fire the experts." *The Daily Oklahoman*, p. A4.

Wolfe, A. (1996, July 22). From Shanghai to Tianjin, China's greatest Olympic resources is clearly its female athletes. *Sports Illustrated*, 152-158

Women Executives Find It Pays to Speak Sports. (1997, September 21). *The Daily Oklahoman*, p. C3.

Xia Zhen. (1998, December 5). Xuanmin zizhu dailing zhengju maixiang xin shidai [Voters's choice leads government and politics into new era]." *China Times* [Online]. Retrieved from: www.content.sina.com/news/chinatimes

Yao hen sha gongkuan chihe xiefeng [The bad practice of eating and drinking by using public money must be stopped]. (1998, November. 18). *Qiaobao* [Online]. Retrieved from: www.dailynews.sina.com/china/chinapress.

Yu zhi qiquo bi xian zhi qijia [To rule the country, it is necessary to rule the family] [Online]. Retrieved from: www.dailynews.sinanet.com/china/chinapress.

Zeng Huiyan. (1996, June 6). Shijie meiyou yiwan liusi youxie zhongguoren que wanjile [The world has not forgot "June 4" but some Chinese have] *Zhijie Zhoukan*,. P. S1.

Index

Albright, Madeleine, 49, 52,
Aristotle, 4, 11,

Ba Dun, 108
Barnathan, J., 43
Beijing (Government), 1, 10, 30, 49, 57-60, 65, 73-85, 94, 117
    relationships with overseas Chinese, 73, 82-86
    relationships with Taiwan, 30-31, 73-82, 94
    relationships with U.S. 10, 117
Beijing opera, 63, 101-109, 115, 133-134
Bloomfield, Frena, 65, 67
Bradley, Bill, 23
Bunning, Jim, 23
business, 1, 3, 8-10, 13-14, 16-25, 39, 41, 43-44, 49-54, 56-57, 60, 63, 67-68, 73, 85, 93, 101, 104-105, 111, 114-117, 119, 121-123
    importance in America, 24-25
    metaphors, 49-54, 121-123
    relationship with politics, 24-25
    relationship with sports, 20-24

Calhoun, K., 21,
Cao Changqing, 106
Cao Zhi-yuan, 82
Carroll, j. B., 7
Casteel, C., 30,
chang (sing), 104-109, 115, 133-134, *See also Beijing opera*
Chang Fang-ming, 9
Chen Shui-bian, 80-81
Chen Hongyi, 77
Chen Ying-ying, 86,
Chenny, Dick, 105
chi, See eating and food
Christopher, Warren, 1, 5-6, 19, 28
Chung, Connie, 63
Cigler, Allen, 25
Clinton, Bill, 1, 5, 12, 24-25, 27-36, 43, 50-52
Clinton, Hillary Rodham, 13, 29, 34, 51

Coakley, J., 21
conceptual system, 3, 5, 8, 19, 31, 119
Confucius, 8, 61-62
Costas, Bob, 20, 83
cultural literacy, x
cultural model(s), 8, 18, 23, 70, 121
culture, 1, 4, 6-10, 13, 24, 31, 55-57, 61-62, 64, 66-68, 71, 74-75, 77, 80, 82-84, 87, 91, 95, 101, 103, 109, 115-116, 119-120
   American, 13-25,
   Chinese, 55-71
   relations with metaphor, 3-11

Deng Xiaoping, 9, 55, 59-60, 65, 70-71, 94, 109
Dole, Bob, 23, 31
driving, 101-103, 111, 115, 119, 123-124
   importance in America, 101-102
   metaphors, 102-103, 123-124

eating (eat) and food, 1, 6-10, 55-56, 64-71, 86- 98, 101, 111-115, 119, 128-131
   importance in China, 64-71
   metaphors, 87-98, 128-131
Eitzen, D.S., 14
Elegant, R.S., 84
Ellingwood, S. 83
Emanatian, M., 5

family, 1, 8-10, 14, 24, 55-64, 73-86, 88, 93-95, 101, 109, 111, 119, 129, 131-133

importance in China, 56-64
   metaphors, 73-86, 131-133
Fan Fu, 93
Fantini, A., 4
Farha, B. 25,
Fauconnier, G., 2
Feingold, Russ, 33-34
Feng Tianyu, 56
Figler, S. K., 21, 23
Fiumara, G.C., 2, 4
Ford, Jack, 46
Friedman, E., 61

Gibbs, R., 2-3, 5, 53
Goatly, A., 2- 3
Goodman, N., 3,
Gorman, J., 21

Hardaway, Francine, 2-3,
Hartman, D., 17, 45
Hatfield, B., 14
Helyar, J., 21
Hill, J., 4
Hirsch, E. D., x
Hollister, Nancy, 50-51
Hu, Jintao, 107-108
Hu, Yaobang, 109
Huang, Annie, 81
Hyde, Henry, 27-28, 32
Hymes, D. 4

Iso-Ahola, S. E., 14

Jack Ford, 46
jia, see family
Jiang Qing, 103
Jiang Zemin, 9, 58-60, 65, 75-76, 106-108
Johnson, M., 2-3, 5, 9, 19
Junichiro Koizumi, 9

Kemp, Jack, 23, 31
Kett, J.. F., x
Kövecses, Z., 4

Lakoff, G., 2-3, 5, 9, 19
Largent, Steve, 23, 27, 34
Lao Zi, 8, 96-97
Latourette, Kenneth Scott, 61, 64
Lee Kuan Yew, 76-77
Lee Teng-hui, 30, 74, 78-80
Li Ao, 81
Li Ge, 86
Lin, Canchu, 71, 86
Lin Chuangcheng, 92
Lin Gan, 92
linguistic
  determinism, 4
  relativity, 4, 7
linguistics, viii
  anthropo-, viii
  socio-, viii
Liu, D., 25, 71, 86
Liu Zhaifu, 92
Livingston, Bob, 31
Loomis, B. B., 25,
Lü Hsiu-lien, 73, 80-81, 86
Lu Xun, 76, 88-92

Ma Dao-rong, 78
Maikovich, A. J. 21
Makiko Tanaka, 9
Mannheim, B., 4
Mao Zedong, 59, 62, 103, 108
mapping (metaphorical process), 4, 18, 22, 119
McGuigan, P. B, 29
Meng Xuan, 30
Michel, Robert, 32

Mo Zi, 56-57, 62
Moise, E., 61
Muhlhausler, Peter, 4, 10

Nance, Roscoe, 15
Naylor, B., 31-32
Nixon, H.L. II, 14
Nonini, D.M., 85

Olson, J., 14
Ong, A., 85
overseas Chinese, 73, 82-86, 94
  (as) China's married-out daughters, 73, 82-86
  Chinese Americans, 83, 94
  tongxiang hui, 82

Palmatier, R. 124-126
Plato, 2,
politicianization, 22, 119

Qian Qichen, 1, 75, 94

Rader, D., 47
Ray, H., 124-126
Roberts, R., 14
Rukeyser, Louis, 18, 39, 41-43
Russert, Tim, 31
Ryun, Jim, 23

Sage, G. H., 14
Schwartz, S. E., 23
Seinfeld, 47
Shiff, R., 5
Socrates, 2
Sowell, Thomas, 52
sports, 2-3, 6-8, 13-24, 27-37, 39-48, 49, 52, 68, 101, 111-113, 119

importance and popularity in America, 13-18
metaphor, 15-19, 27-37, 39-48, 124-128
relationship with business, *see* business
relationship with politics, 21-24
sportsmanization, 22, 119
Starr, Kenneth, 27, 32, 35-36
Starr, Paul, 25
Strickland, Ted, 13, 50-51

Taiwan, 1, 6, 9, 30-31, 58, 70, 73-82, 84-87, 94--95, 113
elections and use of war metaphors, 113
relationships with China, *see* Beijing

Totenburg, Nina, 27, 32-33
Trefil, J. x
Turner, M., 2

Ventura, Jesse, 23
Vogler, C.C., 23

Wahlgren, Eric, 43
Wang, G., 85

Wang Jun, 96-97
Wang Li-juan, 81
Wang Lixiong, 56
Wang Luowang, 93
Wang Yun, 63
Watts, J. C., 23, 49-50
Wayne, Stephen J. 25
Wehrfritz, George, 9
Weiss, A. E., 20-21
Whitaker, G., 21, 23
Whorf, B. L., 4
Wierzbicka, A.,. 4
Wiessler, David, 52
Williams, Walter, 52
Wolfe, A., 7
worldview, 8, 11, 111, 115, 119
Wrigley, 21
Wu, Harry, 84

Xia Zhen, 70

Zeng Huiyan, 6
Zhang Yimou, 68, 84
Zhao Ziyang, 60, 109
Zhou Enlai, 73
Zhou Jiming, 56